MTV
Headbangers Ball

CHAOS AD
ROCK IN THE NINETIES

To all the folks at Roadrunner,

Keep on bringin' the noize!

Cheers,

Steve Beebee

20.6.97

MTV
Headbangers Ball

CHAOS AD
ROCK IN THE NINETIES

Steve Beebee

With an introduction by
Vanessa Warwick

First published in Great Britain by Simon & Schuster Ltd, 1997
A Viacom company

Simon & Schuster Ltd
West Garden Place
Kendal Street
London W2 2AQ

Simon & Schuster Australia
Sydney

A CIP catalogue record for this book is available from the British Library

ISBN 0-684-81920-1

Production manager Aniz Damani
Interior book design by Design/Section, Frome
Colour reproduction by Radstock Reproductions Limited, Midsomer Norton
Printed and bound in Great Britain by Butler & Tanner Limited, Frome and London

Rockin' all over Steve's world

The Gusher's editorial assistant **Steve Beebee** had almost completed his first book when he joined the paper in February. Here he tells what it was like writing about the giants of rock!

YOU wouldn't normally think of Dunchurch as the mecca of rock n'roll, but for several months last year, it felt like just that.

My home was deluged by phone calls and faxes from record companies, TV stations and management gurus from all over the world.

The reason? I had been selected to pen the forthcoming MTV book: 'Chaos AD – Rock In The Nineties,' which is due out next month.

I had already written for Kerrang! magazine for several years, and while I was no stranger to interviewing rock stars, the idea of writing a book was light years away from anything I'd done before. It was the difference between a friendly kick around in the park and the FA Cup Final, replete with extra time and penalties.

MTV producer/presenter Vanessa Warwick, a well known music biz celebrity in her own right, was aware of my past work and, to my astonishment, approached me to take the helm of the Chaos AD project.

The book was to be heavily interview based. I'd be talking to some of the biggest names in rock – Bon Jovi, Aerosmith, Ozzy Osbourne and Def Leppard to name but four. I'd also be talking to the most happening new players on the scene, people like Fear Factory and White Zombie, as well as examining the progress made by women in rock. Courtney Love, Skunk Anansie and Garbage were all high on my list – and not forgetting Vanessa Warwick herself.

Finally, I'd be writing about the people who make the biz buzz – the A&R men, the managers, the promoters and, naturally, the fans

Steve Beebee: Author of a rock music bible about to hit the streets soon. (97May 002DC)

Through Vanessa's manager, Vicki McIvor, Simon and Schuster were chosen as publishers.

Sharing this company with the likes of Ben Elton, HRH The Duchess of York and Hilary Clinton, was yet another honour. Simon and Schuster agreed to a launch throughout the UK and Europe, and later added Australia to the list. Some record companies, like Roadrunner, are very keen to push their artists and assist writers. Certain others, which shall remain nameless, don't appear to care a jot for either, and this was my main obstacle.

Hard work it certainly was, but I never felt under pressure. I was constantly aware of the friendly forces waving my flag.

Vanessa and I had become friends, Vicki

What's more most of the actual interviewees were more than accommodating. I could draw on my previous interviews with Jon Bon Jovi, and my unprecedented visit to his home in New Jersey.

Def Leppard's Joe Elliott postponed a soundcheck to give me the full story, and even gave me the option of calling back for more info. Ozzy Osbourne, in direct opposition to his reputation, is genuine, even minded and a fabulous raconteur.

Chaos AD is released in the UK on June 2, but the promotional wheels are already beginning to turn. Vanessa and I will be doing promotional nights at rock clubs, as well as national press and radio. It's too soon to say where this particular journey will end, but as

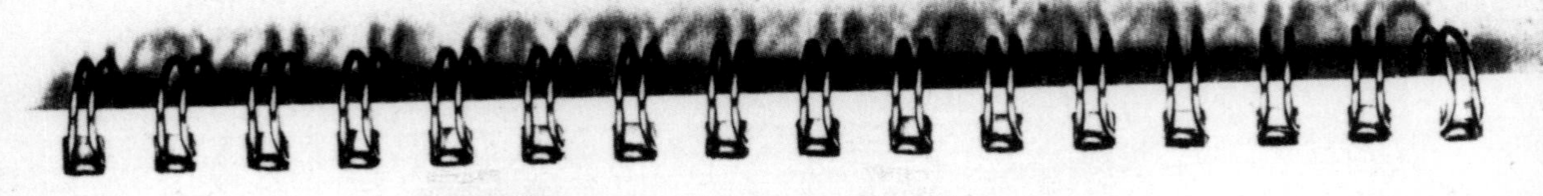

CONTENTS

ACKNOWLEDGMENTS

STEVE BEEBEE

Special thanks to:
Vicki McIvor (Breakthrough Management), Vanessa Warwick, Clare Williams,
Fleur Sarfaty, Richard Godfrey and Jon Critchley (MTV Europe),
Helen Gummer, Ingrid Connell and all at Simon & Schuster.

Thanks also to the following gentlefolk of rock:
Michelle Kerr, Mark Palmer, Marcus Ehresmann, Becky and Kate (Roadrunner);
Gloria Cavalera; Wendy Laister (Collins Management); Julie Quirke;
Sharon Osbourne and Nicole; Liz Morris and co. (Geffen); Sian Thomas and Kas Mercer (Mercury);
Gary Levermore (Tora! Company); Charlie and Sarah (Press Counsel); Tony Linkin (EastWest);
Rob Jefferson (Mushroom); Regine Moylett and all at RMP; Andy Copping; Jon Bon Jovi
for the trip of a lifetime; and Alison Joy whose faith in me all those years ago was priceless…
…and not forgetting all my family, Andy and Michelle Vai, Matt Stevenson,
all the ex-Shotgun mob, plus Mikey, Nails, Ian and
Johnny (Geez United 1, Multimedia Rovers 0).

VANESSA WARWICK

I would like to thank: Anne Newcombe, Brent Hansen, Nancy McDonald, Sam Way,
Marcus Ehresmann, Geoff Gillespie, Tom Miller and Manowar, Joey Huston and Machine Head,
Fear Factory, Simon Horobin and Postbox, Val Janes, Mike Faley, Gloria Cavalera and Sepultura,
Sharon and Ozzy Osbourne, Karen Moore, Vicki McIvor, Gisellah Harvey, Sian Thomas and Def Leppard,
Rod Smallwood and Iron Maiden, Biohazard, Life Of Agony, Magenta Wise, Ronnie Towsend, Skid Row,
Queensryche ('Operation Mindcrime' Rules!), Liz Wells, Sara 'Scoop' Harding, Stuart Cruikshank, Mandi Freeman,
Juliette Moon, Bill Roedy, Mark Brimble, Josh Silver and Type O Negative, Stargazer Cosmetics, Alchemy,
Gloria Butler, Pantera, Gravity Kills, Andy Copping, Nik Moore, Ray Cappo, Korn, Deftones,
Matthew 'Tuds' Archer and most importantly, my dear Mum… for their friendship,
inspiration, and support. Also lots of love and respect to all the bands I have worked
with over the years. Special Thanx to Steve Beebee, Helen Gummer, Julia Sadd,
Liam Sheils, Jason Arnopp without whom…

FOREWORD

James Hetfield

The title of one of my favourite albums, *Live Through This* by Hole, pretty much sums up how strongly I feel about rock and metal music. For Courtney Love, it represents a time that must have been a bad dose of living hell, but for myself, and many of you reading this book, it has a far broader meaning. It's a way of life twenty-four – seven. James Hetfield of Metallica summed it all up when he said, 'Fuckin' metal. It's a way of life beyond just music. It's an attitude!!' Nicely put, mate.

If you feel as strongly as me and James, metal is in your blood and probably in your genes too! It stirs up something for every single one of us at one level or another. What's more, it has survived over the years – from Kiss removing their make-up to putting it back on again! Whatever the category – thrash, death, speed, glam, progressive, industrial, techno, hardcore, grunge – metal will never die, it just re-invents itself, and the attitude lives on to incite more court cases blaming it for everything from teen suicides to forming a pact with him downstairs.

Kiss in Eric Carr, Paul Stanley, Gene Simmons, Bruce Kulick

I was first turned on to rock music because of its impassioned and empowering lyrics, the energy of the music itself, and probably, most of all, because it represented non-conformity. As a confused and rebellious teenager, it proved to be a powerful release from the nightmare of adolescence. It was a way out of boredomsville, where I found the freedom to express myself and be myself – something which has served me in good stead to this very day. At the age of eighteen, I was tearing about on a 750 c.c. motorcycle, bleaching my hair, headbanging the night away to the likes AC/DC, Iron Maiden, Saxon, and Thin Lizzy, and most likely giving my parents a few grey hairs along the way. Well, ten years on, nothing much has changed.

Bruce Dickinson and Steve Harris of Iron Maiden

But while many people enjoy rock music as a hobby, I've been lucky enough to make a career of it through my work at MTV's *Headbangers' Ball*. Over the past five years the programme has gone from strength to strength, and, at the time of writing, is the only rock programmed left on TV in the UK. What's more, in the fast-changing and trendy world of MTV, the fact that it has survived so long on the channel is a testament to the programme's success. Well, you've watched the show, now read the book.

It was always important to me that the book stay true to the spirit and philosophies upheld by its TV counterpart. Well researched, in-depth, and revealing interviews make up the body of many of the chapters you're about to read. The roll call of major artists appearing in this book is longer than an aftershow party guest list for Metallica! There are individual chapters dedicated to the world's biggest stars, the bands who've survived the vagaries of fashions and trends and lived to tell the tale. Artists like Bon Jovi, Ozzy Osbourne and Def Leppard are as relevant today as they've always been.

Pearl Jam

As well as covering the biggest names, *Headbangers' Ball* has always provided a forum for up and coming new talent, and this book holds true to that ethic. Whenever metal has hit a low point, a new band has come along to smash down a few more barriers and remind us why we got into this type of music in the first place. The *Ball* has always been at the forefront of bringing these important new bands to the attention of the masses. It was the first TV programme to introduce you to the likes of Sepultura, Pearl Jam, Blind Melon, Ugly Kid Joe, and more recently Korn, Deftones, Fear Factory, Machine Head and Type O Negative, to name but a very few. So *you* know that *we* know a good band when we hear one! Many of the more recent bands whose causes we have championed are included in chapter nine, New Bands For the Nineties, so get your ears around the psychotic heaviness of Korn and the acute melancholy of Type O Negative to see how the genre is shaping up as we approach the millennium.

Alice In Chains

Nine Inch Nails

As you can see from the names mentioned above, the rock genre has broken through many boundaries in the last few years, largely due to mainstream commercial success of the so-called grunge bands like Pearl Jam, Alice In Chains, Nirvana, and Soundgarden. In the late eighties, every rocker was pretty much stereotyped into the 'cowboy boots, leather jacket, long hair and bandana' club, me included. But the advent of grunge changed all that – the rock genre fragmented, and fans became more open-minded to the new sub-genres being created by bands like Nine Inch Nails, Ministry, Stone Temple Pilots, and Sepultura. In 1996, a typical rock fan might be into everything from Everclear to Extreme and from Marilyn Manson to Motorhead. A very healthy state of affairs, and one which is reflected by the choice of artists for this book, and the weekly video playlist for *Headbangers' Ball*.

It has also given me great personal pleasure to see the advent of so many strong female role models in rock over the past few years. Spearheading the way is, of course, Hole's singer, Courtney Love, one of the most influential figures in music, period. Courtney has taken men on at their own game, proving that women can

Fear Factory

Hole s Courtney Love

indeed rock with attitude – and, to put it bluntly, balls – without compromising on femininity. As you will read later, Courtney is one of the most talked-about women in the world right now, and with good cause. Other women who have come forward with conviction, attitude, and a strong, original image to boot are the likes of Tairrie B. (Manhole), Shirley Manson (Garbage), and Sean Yseult (White Zombie). These rockin' chicks are all fine performers and musicians in their own right, regardless of gender. Tairrie B. in particular has used her role as a platform for women's issues and rights, but, unlike some supporters of the riot grrrl movement, hopes to make men part of the solution,

Manhole l r Scott Ueda, Rico Villasenor Tairrie B, Marcelo Palomino

not the problem. Thanks to these girls, the prejudices against women in rock are slowly but surely being broken down, allowing us to be judged on our individual skills and not on the length of our mini-skirts or the size of our bra cups. Hallelujah!

However, I'm noticing one very worrying trend in the music we know and love. There have recently been several drug-related deaths and scandals. Jonathon Melvion, touring keyboard player with the Smashing Pumpkins, was found dead from a drugs overdose, and couple of weeks later, Phil Anselmo of Pantera nearly went the same way, his heart having stopped beating for four minutes before he was revived in the back of an ambulance. It's a stark reminder of the evil that many musicians find themselves falling prey to. Get real – make no mistake, there is nothing glamorous about drugs. Of course, musicians dying young is nothing new, but with the advent of AIDS in the late eighties, and the risk of it being spread by the sharing of needles, it appeared on the surface that rock music had cleaned up its act. I have see first hand what drug abuse can do to a person, and it's not a pretty sight. So, without wishing to preach, my closing message here takes us full circle to where I started: live through this – don't die through it.

Vanessa Warwick

Thanks for watching the show and enjoy reading the book. Metal lives in the hearts of the musicians who play it and the fans who support them, and, if that all-important attitude was something you could feel, these very pages would probably slap you in the face.

Vanessa Warwick
April 1997

THE HISTORY OF HARD ROCK MUSIC

From the moment it was born, heavy metal was looked on as something to be feared.

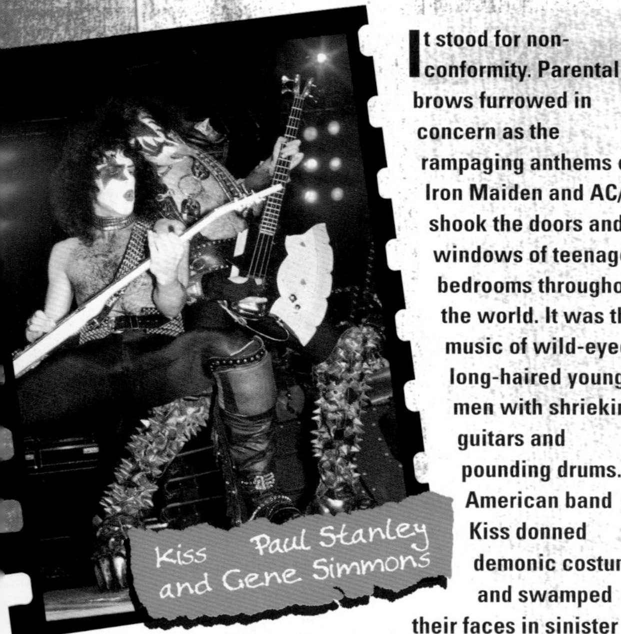

Kiss Paul Stanley and Gene Simmons

It stood for non-conformity. Parental brows furrowed in concern as the rampaging anthems of Iron Maiden and AC/DC shook the doors and windows of teenage bedrooms throughout the world. It was the music of wild-eyed, long-haired young men with shrieking guitars and pounding drums. American band Kiss donned demonic costumes and swamped their faces in sinister black and white war paint. Judas Priest were taken to court, accused of inciting suicide through their music. The lives of AC/DC's Bon Scott, Thin Lizzy's Phil Lynott and Def Leppard's Steve Clark were cut off suddenly, absurdly and tragically: the victims of alcohol and drug abuse. This, we were told, was the devil's music. It was something very bad indeed.

Actually, it was nothing of the sort. Although rock's great standard-bearers have often taken the brunt of media hostility and have walked hand-in-hand with controversy, they have, by and large, enriched people's lives, offering new fashions, forming new traditions and a whole new lifestyle. Sometimes reflecting on everyday dilemmas, and sometimes breathlessly escapist, rock music has been the backdrop for entire generations to plot and reflect upon their lives. For three decades, rock music has ceaselessly developed. Each generation has rejected some parts, embraced others, and added their own unique slant. Rock is virtually a religion.

There was no obvious event that prompted heavy metal's uneasy birth. During the sixties, the Beatles had shown exactly what could be achieved by pop music, and had also demonstrated previously unimaginable creativity within the form. In 1968, John Lennon and George Harrison discovered what would happen if you detuned your guitar slightly and turned the volume up to max. The result was 'Revolution', a song that started out as a typical enough rock 'n' roll-style shuffle, before layers of heavy-duty guitars and strong lyrics were plastered on top. Meanwhile, in America, guitarist Jimi Hendrix had adopted the style of many a black blues legend, before totally reinventing it for his own generation. Hendrix played with apocalyptic power, battering his audiences with seismic waves of sound. Few anticipated that a guitar would ever sound the way that Hendrix made it sound. A new musical consciousness had been tapped into, and millions were entranced.

Music, of course, has always reflected the society from which it has sprung. As the late sixties

A new musical consciousness had been tapped into, and millions were entranced.

Jimi Hendrix Reinventing the art of noise

became the early seventies, young people had started to realise that love was not all they needed after all. Noble though such sentiments were, they had not stopped the American government from dispatching streams of young men to their deaths in Vietnam. One rain-filled weekend in August 1969, at the legendary Woodstock festival, Hendrix wrenched a deconstruction of the American national anthem from his guitar strings, before tearing into his own 'Purple Haze'. It was a one-fingered salute from disgruntled youth to elder Americans, who looked at these tides of long-haired youngsters with anger and disgust. Perhaps, heavy metal was born right there, at that precise moment.

But it appears to have been conceived two years earlier, in the penniless gloom and poverty of downtown Birmingham. One day in 1967, Tony 'Geezer' Butler, a local bass guitarist, knocked on teenager Ozzy Osbourne's front door to see if he wanted to join a group. That group, eventually named Black Sabbath, was probably the first archetypal metal band. Sabbath were a reaction to the frivolous pop ditties dominating the charts, music that was meaningless to four unemployed, unhappy youths from Birmingham. Lead guitarist Tony Iommi patented the dark, grinding riffs that were to inspire countless other metal bands all over the world. Sabbath epitomised the genre. On reflection, the term 'heavy metal' seems tailor made for their style.

At approximately the same time, in neighbouring Stourbridge, ex-Yardbirds guitarist Jimmy Page was getting together with another local singer, Robert Plant. The band, Led Zeppelin, were to be no less legendary than Sabbath. Page alternated thunderous mountains of sound with delicate, Eastern-influenced passages, dominated by Plant's uniquely sexual wail. Zeppelin fired the imagination, constantly experimenting with different sounds and styles. They weren't as bleak or as crazed as Sabbath, and Plant's elevation to sex god status contrasted with Osbourne's thrashing, frantic, wild-man-of-rock image.

A third British band, Deep Purple, also proved pivotal in the way that rock developed. They were once again reliant on a soon to be legendary guitarist and a magnetic frontman, in this case Ritchie Blackmore and Ian Gillan. When Gillan replaced original singer Rod Evans, Deep Purple were able to make the most of their blues influences, while also showing that keyboards could be used prominently without compromising heaviness. The group were the perfect springboard for Blackmore's next group,

Rainbow, and were a crucial reference point for many bands to come, including Whitesnake.

This proud triumvirate of British rock bands established the basic blueprint that legions of acts were to work from in the future. The late sixties had already produced the power blues trio Cream, comprising guitarist Eric Clapton, bassist Jack Bruce and drummer Ginger Baker, not to mention the equally abrasive Yardbirds, with whom both Clapton and Page had cut their teeth. Millions of fans, who had already tuned in to the sound of loud guitars through these bands, catapulted Sabbath, Zeppelin and Purple to the dizzy heights of superstardom. By the mid-seventies, all three were suffering from the excesses of their drug-tainted lifestyle, excesses that had already claimed the life of Jimi Hendrix on 18 September 1970.

Simultaneously, hordes of greasy American college drop-outs were forming their own bands, spewing out aggressive, sleazy garage rock. Detroit's MC5 implored us to 'Kick Out The Jams', while the Stooges, led by the maniacal Iggy Pop, shocked and astonished audiences with their amped-up guitars and lunatic antics. While Blue Cheer drenched themselves in feedback, Free and Humble Pie injected more emotion, through the impassioned blues voices of Paul Rodgers and Steve Marriott. Steppenwolf, mean-while, were the first band to glorify the heavy metal lifestyle, in their classic biker anthem, 'Born To Be Wild'.

Ozzy Osbourne in his Black Sabbath years

Ritchie Blackmore of Deep Purple

Deep Purple in 1973, featuring new vocalist David Coverdale (centre)

American children, some of them the rock stars of the future, hurried to school clutching Kiss lunchboxes.

A self proclaimed God of Thunder — Gene Simmons of Kiss

In the early seventies, rock had diversified into many different streams, and was reaching massive audiences of vastly differing interests and backgrounds. The Stooges paved the way for punk. Sabbath were the forerunners of power metal and thrash. Zeppelin prompted endless epic rock acts to appear, while Free and Deep Purple inspired generations of blues-based bands. Progressive rock bands, such as Yes and King Crimson, attempted to add jazz and classical allusions, eventually influencing bands as varied as Queensryche and Marillion. To cope with the diversification of rock and the acute interest therein, a wide range of music papers and magazines came into existence, reflecting the youth culture of the day and attempting to influence the future. Several, such as *New Musical Express*, *Melody Maker* and *Rolling Stone*, still survive.

Rock music was forged in the fire of political and social unrest, poverty, boredom and frustration. Paganism, the occult, drugs and seedy sex were common subject matter. The time had come for something brighter, more frivolous and fun. The time had come for glam rock. As the likes of Gary Glitter and Suzi Quatro stomped all over the pop chart, a rock equivalent was urgently required. Pretty soon there was a glut of glam or glam-influenced rock bands from both sides of the Atlantic. The emphasis was on outrageous clothing and footwear, gaudy make-up, and bouncy, bubbly anthems with memorable melodies. British bands like Slade and the Sweet blasted out a rush of turbocharged party rock with titles like 'Cum On Feel the Noize' and 'Ballroom Blitz'. Queen, who were to modify the genre by giving far greater attention to musicality, were launched by EMI records in 1973, and were to prove one of the most durable acts produced by the glam genre.

American bands of the day displayed a more destructive, sinister edge. Alice Cooper was the first to dress outrageously and wear lipstick in the name of theatricality, but for Cooper, the effect was not so much glamorous as macabre. Cooper endeavoured to shock, developing a kind of horror theatre in which to perform his searing teen anthems. The hugely influential but totally self-destructive New York Dolls wore high heels and tacky leather outfits to complement their loose, rebellious sleaze. In terms of outrage, theatricality and the provoking of sheer audience adoration, however, there was one American rock band who stood head and shoulders above all others: Kiss.

Issuing their eponymous debut album in 1974, the four members of Kiss each assumed the identity of a bizarre science fiction character, wearing individual black and white face paint, and a succession of astonishing costumes. Frontman Paul Stanley, bassist Gene Simmons, guitarist Ace Frehley, and drummer Peter Criss added to the intrigue by never allowing themselves to be photographed without their make-up and stage outfits in place. They issued a series of classic albums, including *Destroyer* and *Love Gun*, and American youth culture treated them as gods. By 1977, Kiss were staging vast theatrical spectacles, with hitherto inconceivable pyrotechnics and effects. American children, some of them the rock stars of the future, hurried to school clutching Kiss lunchboxes. Although the band removed their make-up in 1983 and consequently lost much of their appeal, they remain one of the most influential bands in rock history. Indeed, in 1996 Kiss reformed their original make-up spattered line-up and regained their former glory.

The ascendancy of Kiss was rapid enough to have shaken rock to its very foundations. Popular British bands like UFO and Uriah Heep seemed tame and pedestrian in comparison. Suddenly, rock needed to be raunchy and bombastic; a little bit dangerous to succeed. Aerosmith (see chapter five) were one of the main beneficiaries. Initially looked on as America's version of the Rolling Stones, the Boston-based band now issued two seminal albums, *Toys in the Attic* (1975) and *Rocks* (1976), and were immediately propelled to stardom. AC/DC also began their meteoric rise, clubbing listeners with ardent, pummelling riffs and high-octane vocals. Legendary frontman Bon Scott and guitarist Angus Young, clad in school uniform, provided a unique visual focus that helped the band to amass a huge cult following. AC/DC were to record such influential albums as *High Voltage* and *Let There Be Rock*. Meanwhile, the charismatic Phil Lynott, one of the most talented and sensitive songwriters of his generation, also saw his band, Thin Lizzy, achieve international success. Lizzy will probably be best remembered for the seminal *Jailbait* album. The influence of both bands cannot be overstated

In the years 1976–9, the rock world was devastated by the arrival of punk. The rock star idiom was wholeheartedly rejected as a new wave of young bands offered the antithesis to inflated arena rock. Punk stripped away all the unnecessary frills and replaced them with raw, honest muscle. It was aggressive, simplistic music with very few chords, absolutely no finesse, but seemingly boundless energy. Most importantly of all, it was the music of a new, younger breed of bands who were sick of listening to the ageing rock of their elder siblings and parents. Punk was intent on hailing its own generation and no other.

Its most notorious exponents, the Sex Pistols, abided by a philosophy set out for them by their clever manager, Malcolm McLaren. Established rock bands were labelled 'boring old hippies', and it was suggested that we 'set light to them', rubbishing and destroying every institution that had gone before, perhaps creating anarchy. At the insistence of McLaren, the Pistols undertook a series of publicity stunts, each designed to cause as much outrage and controversy as possible. In their desire to establish irreconcilable generation gaps and parent–child friction, they were wholly successful. The Sex Pistols were the band that parents loved to hate. Johnny Rotten and Sid Vicious were public anti-heroes, Vicious ending his short career in typically graphic style by stabbing his girlfriend, Nancy Spungen, to death, and dying from a drugs overdose before he could be convicted of her murder.

The Ramones

The music media became infatuated with the new movement, largely because it proved the true power of youth culture, and gave it a definite voice. Punk, which included such bands as the Damned, the Clash, the Ramones and the Dead Kennedys, was to play a major role in the revitalisation of heavy rock over the next two decades. Rock veered away from endless indulgent soloing and mystical lyrics, and instead favoured a shorter, more direct format, with a new social and political lyrical slant. In the wake of punk, an ever greater number of sub-cultures appeared, often crossing over, creating an endless slew of new music. Rock was not, as McLaren intended, destroyed, but exorcised of its demons and rejuvenated.

Inevitably though, many long-established bands suffered as the new order underlined its authority. Cracks appeared within the ranks of Kiss, and in 1979, Ozzy Osbourne (see chapter six) left Black Sabbath, putting a permanent end to the classic original line-up. Led Zeppelin's star was also on the wane and Deep Purple had already called it a day, albeit temporarily. The following year, Zeppelin were finished, unable to continue after the death of drummer John Bonham. AC/DC's Bon Scott was another victim of seventies' excess, though the Antipodean rockers were to continue, recruiting British-born singer Brian Johnson as his replacement.

More positively, Van Halen exploded on to an American market hungry for new, innovative bands. Their music was dubbed 'atomic punk' because it combined the brash, direct bombast of punk with expert musicianship and visual flamboyance. Extrovert singer David Lee Roth became the role model for aspiring frontmen all over the world, while Eddie Van Halen's incendiary soloing added a new dimension to what could be achieved with a guitar. Heavy metal had entered a new era, and at the turn of the decade a surge of new British talent took the genre by storm.

David Lee Roth

Eddie Van Halen

N W O B H M

This movement, dubbed the New Wave of British Heavy Metal (NWOBHM) by *Sounds* critic Geoff Barton, resulted in a plethora of new signings, and the emergence of similar developments in America, Europe and the Far East.

NWOBHM included such names as Diamond Head, Raven, Angelwitch, Demon and Praying Mantis, but its primary exponents were

Iron Maiden

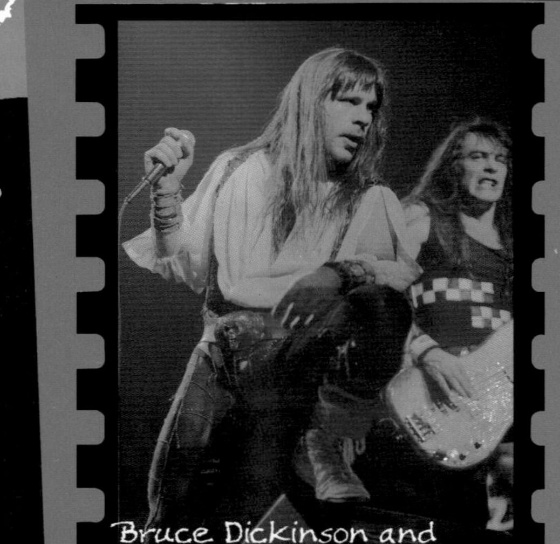

Bruce Dickinson and Steve Harris of Iron Maiden

undoubtedly Iron Maiden, Def Leppard (see chapter three) and Saxon. It was hoped that this new, three-pronged attack of British rock would take metal screaming into the next decade, as Sabbath, Zeppelin and Purple had done previously. Bands involved in the NWOBHM traditionally performed loud, energetic sets with intricate guitar solos, pounding bass lines and raucous, instantly memorable hooks. The tendency to play in small clubs and pubs, developing a fan base at grass roots level, allied the movement closely with punk. The studs and the leather remained, but suddenly it was advisable to have long hair again.

During the following years, both Iron Maiden and Def Leppard gradually refined their musical mannerisms, the former developing a grandiose, epic style, and the latter eschewing their early influences in favour of superbly orchestrated, harmony-led pop rock. In the decades that followed, Iron Maiden were to dominate the UK charts with their aggressive metal anthems, even scoring a Number One hit single with 'Bring Your Daughter... to the Slaughter'. Maiden also managed to headline Donington twice, in 1988 and 1991. Saxon, however, stayed true to their NWOBHM roots, and by 1990 had virtually disappeared from view. Media derision of bands who were perceived not to have evolved stylistically made longevity difficult for many of NWOBHM's early heroes. Even the greatly respected Diamond Head, cited as an influence by Metallica and Queensryche, were unable to sustain their success.

However, several bands that had survived the seventies found the new movement very much to their liking. Before too long, certain more experienced bands were matching the youngsters at their own game. Amongst them were Judas Priest, Twisted Sister, Motorhead and the lighter, more esoteric Magnum, all groups that had debuted in the early or mid-seventies. For the first time, female bands such as the British Girlschool and Rock Goddess emerged from the shadows of their male counterparts. In the US, the Runaways, a band that featured both Lita Ford and Joan Jett, are regarded as the first true standard-bearers for women in metal. Although similar acts tended to be embraced purely for their novelty factor, and were consequently unable to reap massive success, the Runaways made the first of many great strides women were to make in a heavily male-dominated environment. Like punk before it, NWOBHM had unblocked rock's arteries, and had added many fresh perspectives and colours to the overall picture.

The birth of MTV on 1 August 1981 acted as a catalyst for the eighties' rock boom. From this date onwards, the business of being in music had been changed for ever. In pop, only videogenic bands like Duran Duran and the Human League could hope to have a serious chart impact. By 1986, the idea of releasing a single without a promotional video to accompany it was tantamount to commercial suicide. The advent of video opened many new doors for rock and pop groups alike. Record companies now had new methods of promoting their artists, and a greater emphasis on visual as well as aural presentation was the inevitable outcome. MTV helped to launch Def Leppard in America, where they achieved considerable success. As a consequence of this success, Geoff Barton, the critic who had championed the band in Britain, had already pondered whether the Leppard had 'changed its spots'.

Lita Ford

The eighties also provided a platform for the general ascendancy of metal sets from all parts of Europe. Germany and Scandinavia proved to be particularly fertile territories for new talent. Biggest of all were the Scorpions. Already known in the seventies for their raw but professional style, the new decade saw them upgraded into an international act of immense repute. With Klaus Meine's distinctive vocal style and the serrated, muscle-bound riffing of guitarists Rudolf Schenker and Matthias Jabs, the Scorpions soon became one of the most influential rock bands on the world scene. The legendary *Love At First Sting* album was released in 1984 and included such choice Scorpion cuts as 'Rock You Like a Hurricane', 'Coming Home' and the timeless ballad 'Still Loving You'. The band followed up this release in 1985 with *Worldwide Live*, a double live album that underlined their international repute.

In the Scorpions' wake came a steady stream of talented professional German bands. Helloween proved to be one of the more successful. Their early albums followed in the footsteps of Iron Maiden, adding a touch of their own finesse and polish. Despite an ever-changing line-up, the band survived and remain a popular European attraction to this day. Bonfire added a more radio-friendly variation on the theme, while the female-fronted Warlock also gained recognition for their aggressive, fuel-injected brand of mayhem. Indeed Warlock singer Doro Pesch was a leading light for women in rock for several years, jostling with American solo artist Lita Ford (ex-Runaways) for top spot.

> ...the rock world turned to Hollywood, the centre of all that was glamorous and hedonistic...

The ultra-commercial Europe, hailing from Sweden, set the charts alight all over the continent and beyond. Dismissed by some as 'pretty boys', they were briefly as popular as Bon Jovi. Inspired by their success, other melodic Scandinavian bands, such as Treat, Stage Dolls and Alien, enjoyed their fifteen minutes of fame. Sweden's output was not limited solely to soft rock, however, as the frighteningly heavy Candlemass illustrated in the late eighties. The release of *Nightfall*, with its controlled power and portentous ambience, inspired many of the popular doom metal bands today, including Paradise Lost and My Dying Bride. The eighties was the decade when the European scene came of age.

With rock exploding into the charts on both sides of the Atlantic, a myriad of separate styles developed. The media gleefully attempted to categorise bands, filing them as thrash, sleaze, funk metal, techno metal, power metal, doom metal, grindcore, death metal, Christian metal and beyond. Now that image was all-important, and the eighties' predatory hunger for affluence and living it up had set in, the rock world turned to Hollywood, the centre of all that was glamorous and hedonistic, for inspiration. The outrageous Mötley Crüe, with their bouffant hairstyles, lipstick and sexed-up party anthems, were the first of a vast tide of similar bands. Los Angeles became the mecca of the new wave of glam rock. Record company talent scouts flocked to LA's Sunset Strip where spruced up, larger-than-life wannabes performed at clubs like the Roxy and the Whisky every night.

Mötley Crüe

After Mötley Crüe, Ratt and W.A.S.P. had achieved both record sales and notoriety, aspiring rock stars of a similar ilk relocated to LA *en masse*. An astonishing glut of bands was signed, completely saturating the market. Guns N'Roses (see chapter four) and Poison were to become superstars. The majority were forgotten very quickly. It was the riotous Guns N'Roses, in particular, who were to have such a profound effect on rock over the next few years, influencing everything from music to fashion on the strength of one classic album, *Appetite For Destruction*. So many West Coast bands were signed that the entire scene had burnt out by 1990.

As a contrast to glam, thrash and speed metal offered an alternative to those who sought harder, more aggressive music. Metallica (see chapter seven) proved to be the most commercially successful, followed by Slayer, Anthrax and Megadeth. The Bay Area of San Francisco was considered the most fertile zone for signing new bands, and was almost treated as the thrash equivalent of Sunset Strip. Almost single-handedly, Metallica developed the genre and attained widespread commercial acceptance for

Mötley Crüe on the 'Girls Girls Girls' tour

what was once perceived as 'alternative' or 'underground' music. This was by no means the last example of this type of occurrence.

Although metal was now reaching a wider audience than ever before, the undisputed champions of chart-bound rock were Bon Jovi (see chapter two). The New Jersey band were an indirect product of the LA glam movement, but had the added integrity conferred by Aerosmith and Thin Lizzy influences in their genes. More importantly, their music had an integral pop element, whilst their image was not as bizarre or threatening as that of Mötley Crüe.

By 1987, they were the biggest rock group in existence, and for them, it was only the beginning. Bon Jovi crossed over into the pop market, effectively opening the floodgates for many other bands. Millions of fans throughout the world, who would never have considered the likes of Iron Maiden and Motorhead a few years before, were now turned on to rock in all its myriad forms.

Bands that could combine expert melodic rock with an attractive, vibrant image, were welcomed in their hordes. Europe scored an international Number One single with 'The Final Countdown', a pomp-filled rhapsody with signature keyboard phrases. Def Leppard were now able to emulate their Stateside success at home. Even relative old-timers like Kiss, Aerosmith and Whitesnake were suddenly in demand. Kiss gained their biggest UK hit ever with 'Crazy, Crazy Nights', while Aerosmith albums *Permanent Vacation* (1987) and *Pump* (1989) sold by the truck-load. Interest in Kiss and Aerosmith had been revived by Bon Jovi and Guns N'Roses, the two biggest rock bands of the day, who cited both as prominent influences. Meanwhile, Whitesnake, who had initially been formed by one-time Deep Purple singer David Coverdale, and had sounded much the same, now brilliantly reinvented themselves, combining elements of classic seventies rock with eighties production values and sensuous video imagery.

Motorhead's inimitable Lemmy

The late eighties also bore witness to another wave of up and coming British bands. This time, the bands in question were disparate in style and influence, and could not be summed up by a restrictive category like NWOBHM. Little Angels aimed for the Bon Jovi market, while the Quireboys attempted to revive interest in the Faces and the Rolling Stones. Wolfsbane and the Almighty aimed for a harder, more metal-oriented approach, and Thunder breathed new life into the old British tradition of blues-based heavy rock. European bands attempting to mimic LA's now crumbling glam movement were met with media derision. Only Tigertailz managed to amass any kind of following, but even they came to fruition rather too late.

Gru

Pearl Jam

There's a new kind of music coming.

As the eighties rolled into the nineties, American bands could be slotted into two distinct categories. There were those that wished to cling on to the receding bandwagon of eighties rock, and those who wished to experiment. Vixen, despite their formulaic melodic rock, were one of the first significant all-female bands, while Skid Row, Extreme and Warrant also registered impressive sales. However, the scene was becoming tired and stale. Audiences and artists alike began to search for alternatives to the increasingly pompous and predictable rock music dominating the airwaves. The rise of black, or black-influenced, groups began. Living Color, the Dan Reed Network, the Red Hot Chili Peppers and King's X incorporated funk, pop, jazz and reggae influences. They defied pigeonholing by remaining utterly diverse, and, with their more thoughtful lyrics, encouraged fans to take a more responsible attitude to the world around them. It was all a far cry from the sexist and increasingly clichéd outlook of many a mainstream rock act.

In 1991, the world of rock was hit by a cyclone. Kory Clarke, of New York punk metallers Warrior Soul, was the first to note what was going on. As early as March 1990, the prophetic Clarke told *Kerrang!* writer Phil Wilding, 'I think we're post-metal. There's a new kind of music coming. It's got different values. Tints of grey, shadows…' To the amusement of some, Clarke predicted the genocide of dumb, party metal; of bands like Winger and Warrant, bands that were then selling millions of albums. The following year, as the music industry's focus switched to rainy Seattle, he was proved unnervingly accurate.

Grunge was the post-metal Clarke had referred to, and its prime mover, Nirvana, detonated on to the scene like a dozen nuclear warheads, debunking nearly all the leading lights of corporate rock and forcing them underground. In a movement that echoed the American garage rock of the late sixties and the British punk invasion of 1976–9, Seattle

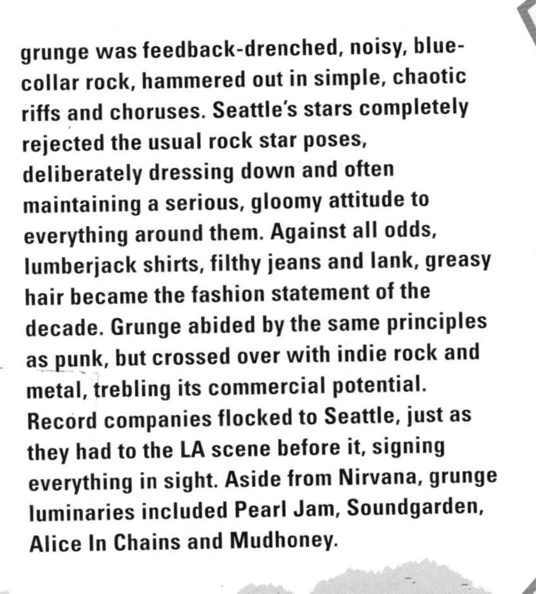

grunge was feedback-drenched, noisy, blue-collar rock, hammered out in simple, chaotic riffs and choruses. Seattle's stars completely rejected the usual rock star poses, deliberately dressing down and often maintaining a serious, gloomy attitude to everything around them. Against all odds, lumberjack shirts, filthy jeans and lank, greasy hair became the fashion statement of the decade. Grunge abided by the same principles as punk, but crossed over with indie rock and metal, trebling its commercial potential. Record companies flocked to Seattle, just as they had to the LA scene before it, signing everything in sight. Aside from Nirvana, grunge luminaries included Pearl Jam, Soundgarden, Alice In Chains and Mudhoney.

nge

In retrospect, it is not difficult to see why grunge happened. Eighties youth was buoyed by dreams of affluence and success, excited at the prospects offered by the new Tory government in Britain, and by the Reagan and Bush administrations in America. Teenagers in the nineties discovered that academic achievement was no guarantee of employment, let alone riches. Gender roles had become blurred, AIDS was a major issue, drugs and rave culture became prevalent along with gang warfare, racial disharmony and controversial Western involvement in Middle Eastern conflicts.

Soundgarden's Frontman
Chris Cornell

Nine Inch Nails

L7

White Zombie

Young people felt that they faced an uncertain future in a confusing, troubled society. Nirvana's Kurt Cobain, the kingpin of teen angst, was unfairly looked on as the voice of a new generation. Whilst this might have once been true of John Lennon, Cobain could provide no easy answers for the millions that idolised him. He could, however, scream out in empathy, mirroring the disorder and frustration around him. The bright spotlight of fame, and the responsibility that he felt it entailed, proved too much for Cobain, who took his own life in April 1994.

This shattering tragedy deeply affected almost everyone involved in rock music, and marked the end of Seattle's tenure as the hotbed of new talent. It did not, however, halt the wave of so-called alternative metal, which continued to sub-divide and win favour amongst young audiences. Stone Temple Pilots, Soul Asylum and Smashing Pumpkins played a more dynamic, emotionally enhanced version of grunge, with each accounting for millions of album sales. Roadrunner, an independent record company, gained immense credibility by signing a host of innovative new bands, amongst them Dog Eat Dog, Machine Head, Type O Negative, Fear Factory and Brazilian metallers Sepultura (see chapter eight). Meanwhile, Texan rockers Pantera also provided a heavier, less commercial alternative to Metallica.

Since Cobain's death, Pearl Jam, in particular, continued to push grunge into the mainstream. Frontman Eddie Vedder, with his thoughtful lyrics and tremendous stage presence, has become a pivotal force in the band, despite his shunning the limelight. With a new album, *No Code*, in the bag, Pearl Jam show no signs of relinquishing their dominance.

Meanwhile, industrial metal has attempted to represent the confusion of nineties society by using machines and computers to create complex waves of sound. By far the greatest exponent of this trend was Trent Reznor's brainchild, Nine Inch Nails, whose intensely theatrical shows replete with sado-masochistic imagery made them one of the most popular live acts in the world. Along with that of Ministry,

Reznor's influence was felt far and wide, with many bands choosing to add industrial edges to their output. This generally dark and menacing music, with its trademark distortion on the vocals, created such bands as Fear Factory, Stabbing Westward and Misery Loves Co. More significantly, it played a major part in the multi-platinum success of shock rockers White Zombie.

Female or female-fronted bands were no longer marginalised, or viewed as objects of titillation, and contributed greatly to the development of the genre. Spearheading the movement, somewhat inevitably, was Hole, the band fronted by Kurt Cobain's widow, Courtney Love. L7 and Babes In Toyland were two other bands of consequence. Many female bands were labelled as Riot Grrrls, in an attempt to describe their aggressive punk-and grunge-influenced sounds. Most bands thus described also opted for strong feminist messages in their lyrics, and reinforced their brash image by wearing combat boots and army fatigues in place of the stiletto heels and skin-tight leather of earlier bands like Vixen. Courtney Love, however, insisted that it was not necessary for women to dress down to play powerful music or to be artistically credible. Despite allowing herself to become embroiled in endless controversy, she has never altered her image or compromised her ideals. Many women have given vent to their own feelings, including Manhole's outspoken Tairrie B, and Swedish grunge band Drain.

The mid-nineties has also witnessed the so-called second coming of punk. Ironically, most of the bands involved have merely incorporated certain values of punk, rather than the style of the actual music. Many fans who remember the Sex Pistols and the Damned have expressed exasperation at the use of the word punk to label present-day bands like Offspring. Whatever the objection of older fans, German band Die Toten Hosen saw their fortunes improve considerably under the new regime, and fellow-Europeans H-Blockx also saw commercial success, and even toured with Bon Jovi.

Hole s Courtney Love

Nirvana s Kurt Cobain

Green Day, the most successful example of the current crop, have remarkably little in common with the Sex Pistols, other than the brevity and simplicity of their material. The main reason for their success stems from their provision of a happier, more carefree alternative to grunge, without compromising the energy and intensity that fans have grown accustomed to. Certainly, the Stateside success of Green Day has been little short of phenomenal, and has naturally given the green light to an onslaught of similar acts, including Offspring, Rancid and NOFX. It's quirky, positive music, with the emphasis shifted to fun rather than anger. In this respect, grunge can be said to have had more in common with first-wave punk than what passes for punk today.

During 1995 and '96, Britain was again rapidly producing promising young rock acts. Terrorvision have responded gleefully to the brighter, more vibrant sounds coming from America with their own brand of powerful punk- and pop-flavoured rock. The Wildhearts have won endless acclaim for the way they have laid sweet pop harmonies on to blisteringly heavy song structures, while Paradise Lost have kept traditional British metal's flag flying. Skin, meanwhile, have continued the tradition of Thunder and Whitesnake, while Skunk Anansie, Honeycrack, Swear, 3 Colours Red and Northern Ireland's Therapy? currently rejoice in three-minute dynamics, and, above all, brilliant songs. Like all movements, several faceless post-grunge bandwagon jumpers have also tagged along for the ride, but the overall feeling has been one of rejuvenation, a fresh start for a heritage rich in rock tradition. *Kerrang!* editor Phil Alexander enthusiastically christened the movement 'Britrock'.

Over the years, and there have been nearly thirty of them, rock has changed in many different ways. Styles have fused and multiplied like living organisms. The term 'heavy metal', so appropriate in the days when Black Sabbath and Led Zeppelin were surfacing from rock's primeval mire, now seems almost redundant. Are Bon Jovi heavy metal? Are Nine Inch Nails? Were Nirvana? At the end of the day, mere labels are of minimal value. The fact that rock has branched out in so many directions can only be healthy, and accounts for its continued survival.

After almost three decades of rock history, the genre continues to develop, perpetually dividing and sub-dividing. It has never failed to fascinate and frustrate those who claim allegiance to it. Rock fans have continued to plead the cause of their favourite bands, in the classroom, in the work place, or in the pub. We have witnessed and documented the lives of our heroes. We have surfed the high waves of their triumphs. Iron Maiden reaching Number One in the UK singles chart. Def Leppard drummer Rick Allen's successful comeback after losing an arm in a car accident. The victories of Aerosmith and Ozzy Osbourne over drug addiction. Equally, we have suffered their tragedies and keenly felt their loss. Randy Rhoads, Bon Scott, Phil Lynott, John Bonham, Eric Carr, Sid Vicious, Kurt Cobain, Freddie Mercury, Steve Clark, Cliff Burton, Shannon Hoon, Jimi Hendrix. All gone.

The stars, be they dead or alive, shining or waning, have affected us in all manner of ways. No matter where our particular allegiance lies, their music has already reached out to touch us. Tomorrow, like yesterday and today, we will walk hand in hand with it.

Thin Lizzy's Phil Lynott died 4 January 1986

We have witnessed and documented the lives of our heroes.

Sex Pistols

Ozzy Osbourne

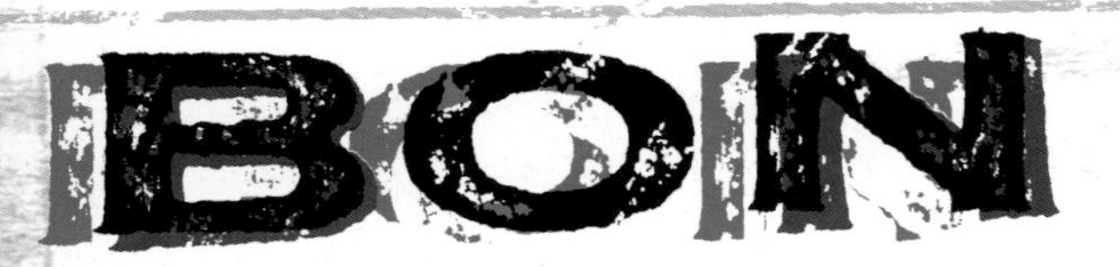

When the drought was at its worst, along came Bon Jovi to replenish the reservoir. Like rock's answer to Luke Skywalker or Wyatt Earp, they shot the bad guys, got the girl and rode off into the sunset. By popularising rock music, New Jersey's finest simply threw open the doors and beckoned in a cast of millions to enjoy the party. They trimmed away rock's fat, stripping and burning its more ridiculous elements, making it available to all. Consequently, numerous other rock acts woke up to find the world at their feet, with even the likes of Metallica and Anthrax Top Twenty bound.

Bon Jovi are the people's band. They left metal's drug-crazed harbingers of doom to their own thing, instead offering us songs of hope and unity, songs about ordinary people staring life full in the face. Their accessible good looks and passionate songwriting sent seismic shivers through rock's entire infrastructure. Their influence not only on music, but on people's lives, cannot be overstated. People have seen their own struggles reflected in songs like 'Keep the Faith', 'Livin' on a Prayer' and 'Blood on Blood'. People who absorbed the sincerity and warmth of Bon Jovi's music have sewn it into the fabric of their day to day life. Bands like Bon Jovi will come along once in a lifetime. If you're lucky.

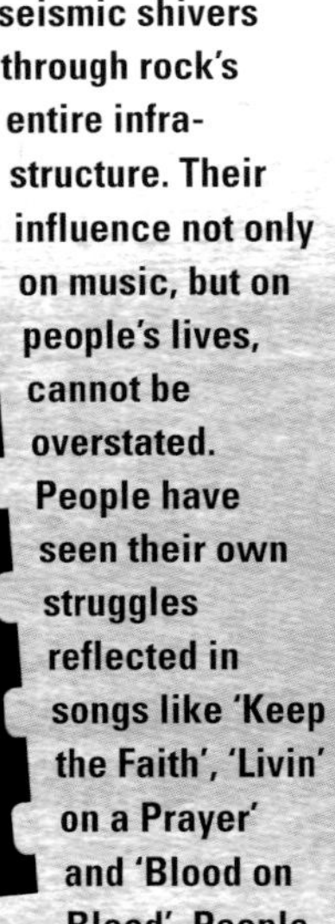

Jon Bon Jovi

'As a songwriter, it's very satisfying to hear that what I do has had such an effect on people,' says Jon Bon Jovi emphatically. 'That, to me, was the ultimate goal. It all came home to me once, when I met this guy who plays quarterback for the New England Patriots. I felt like a little kid waiting to meet him, but to my amazement it turned out that he was a massive Bon Jovi fan. I was nervous about meeting him, so it felt really weird for me to give him my autograph. Suddenly, it started to make sense. The quarterback was only twenty-one years old, and every young person has heroes. What would we do without them?'

Jon was born on 2 March 1962 in Perth Amboy, New Jersey, and spent his childhood in Sayreville, a working class suburb of the same state. The eldest of three brothers, Jon acquired his first guitar at the age of seven, and took lessons from a local music teacher, Al Parinello. His first band was a short lived venture called Raze, which spectacularly finished last in a school talent contest. It was at Sayreville High, however, that Jon became friends with David Rashbaum, a young man of Jon's own age who had been trained as a classical pianist. Rashbaum was later to change his surname to Bryan and become Bon Jovi's full-time keyboard player.

'It's a life force when you first pick up a guitar and get that rush, that aspiration to take on the world and conquer it,' says Jon. 'There's no greater feeling for me than to write songs that people like; but when the machine comes down and tries to eat you up, it can kill you. In rock 'n' roll, you can get a lobotomy without realising what's happening.'

The duo assembled a ten-piece R&B outfit called Atlantic City Expressway, and started gigging at local clubs. Jon worked in a shoe shop to help

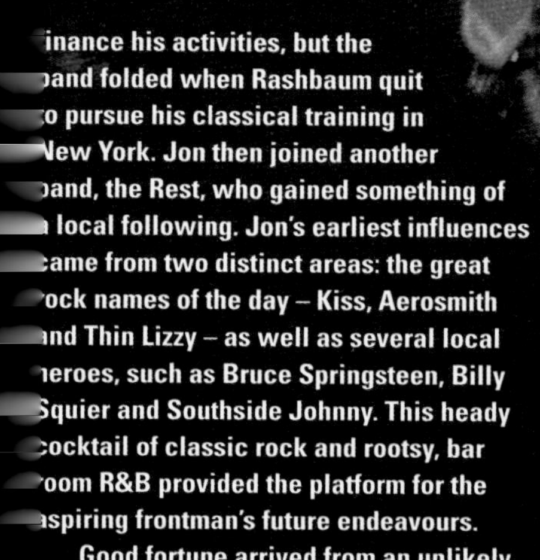

finance his activities, but the band folded when Rashbaum quit to pursue his classical training in New York. Jon then joined another band, the Rest, who gained something of a local following. Jon's earliest influences came from two distinct areas: the great rock names of the day – Kiss, Aerosmith and Thin Lizzy – as well as several local heroes, such as Bruce Springsteen, Billy Squier and Southside Johnny. This heady cocktail of classic rock and rootsy, bar room R&B provided the platform for the aspiring frontman's future endeavours.

Good fortune arrived from an unlikely source. Jon's second cousin, Tony Bongiovi, owned New York's Power Station Studios, and took Jon on as a cleaner and errand boy. In return, Jon got to learn about the music industry and recording processes, and was able to cut his own demo tapes after finishing his chores. Pretty soon, Jon formed a new band called the Wild Ones, and recorded a few songs.

When the drought was at its worst, along came Bon Jovi to replenish the reservoir. Like rock's answer to Luke Skywalker or Wyatt Earp...

1 July 1983. Respected session bassist Alec John Such was recruited, and he, in turn, recommended drummer Tico Torres, already a veteran of several moderately successful bands. Guitarist Richie Sambora (born in Woodbridge, New Jersey on 11 July 1959) was the last to join. Sambora remains to this day a perpetually cheerful, uncomplicated character with a fine sense of humour.

'I was named after a used-car parking lot!' admits Sambora. 'You see, my mom was a cheerleader and my dad was a "greaser", kinda like Fonzie from *Happy Days*, but not as goofy. They were obsessed by old cars and bikes, and there was a used-car lot across the way which was like a paradise for my dad. The place was called Richards, and the rest is history. But I don't mind, it's a good name – strong, sturdy and reliable.'

Equally importantly, Sambora also had a deep love of music, a quality that endeared him immediately to Jon. Not only was he one of the finest rock guitarists around, but he could also claim allegiance to the more emotional qualities of musicians like Eric Clapton and Stevie Ray Vaughan. Jon knew that Richie was undoubtedly in it for the long haul.

One of them, 'Runaway', caught Tony's attention. The song was entered for a local radio competition, and after winning the regional heat, it appeared on a compilation album put out by the radio station. With Rashbaum back on board, the name 'Wild Ones' was dropped in favour of 'Bon Jovi', because Jon was effectively viewed as a solo artist. The compilation album raised record company eyebrows, and a number of major labels expressed interest in the young rocker from New Jersey.

It was PolyGram's Derek Schulman who eventually signed what was to become the biggest rock act in the world, gaining Jon's signature on

Bon Jovi played at every club that would have them, till PolyGram threw them in at the deep end, offering them a support slot with ZZ Top at New York's famous Madison Square Garden. It was a stressful time for all, but an important learning process nonetheless.

Unsurprisingly, Bon Jovi recorded their self-titled debut album at the Power Station, with Tony Bongiovi and his more experienced partner Lance Quinn at the production helm. It was a nervous, erratic album that combined some great moments with some thoroughly mediocre ones. 'Runaway', however, steered it in the right direction. Despite being accompanied by an appalling video, the song nevertheless brought Bon Jovi their first U.S. hit single, peaking at Number 39. On the weight of similar tracks, such as the precise, effective 'Breakout' and the good-time, party shebang of 'Get Ready', the album was well received by the media, and became something of a cult classic in hard rock circles.

On the strength of the single, ironically the very same song that had won Bon Jovi their deal, they set off on tour in America, supporting a number of big-name acts. They also made their debut on British soil, supporting rock legends Kiss. By this time, they were scaling their particular learning curve at a startling rate, and left British audiences with much to remember. Japanese audiences also savoured their first taste of the band.

'To be honest, our longevity has been more a result of persistence than clever forward thinking,' says a modest Jon. 'In those early days, we just looked at everyone and said, "Sorry, but we're still gonna be here next year, and the year after that, and if you don't like our current record then we'll soon make another!"'

Bon Jovi were a rapidly developing talent, having already attained a respectable degree of success. Rather than giving fans a chance to forget about the band, it was decided to press on immediately with a second album. In retrospect, this was an unwise move. The album, *7800 Degrees Fahrenheit*, was released in April 1985, barely a year after its predecessor. Clearly, anticipation of a second Bon Jovi album, and that all-important 'buzz' factor, had not been given time to develop, and despite the fact that the new record was a vast improvement on the last, it was panned by the critics. In terms of production, performance and songwriting, *7800 Degrees Fahrenheit* buried the first album. 'In and Out of Love' and the dramatic 'Tokyo Road' were sharp, dynamic rockers, totally in synch with the times. 'Silent Night' and 'Only Lonely' were moodier, more emotional passion plays, displaying a new angle to Bon Jovi's songwriting. Not all the songs were great, but the album should nevertheless have been seen as a significant step forward.

As it happened, sales were initially very slow. It was only down to Bon Jovi's application as a live act that the situation was rescued. Jovi hit the American road with Los Angeles' glam rockers Ratt, then at the peak of their powers. Under pressure to succeed, Bon Jovi delivered a string of taut, defiant performances, emphatically eclipsing the headliners.

'Back in 1985, all the Los Angeles bands were doing well and we weren't,' recalls Jon. 'For about a minute we believed that all we needed for success was fancy clothes. Opening for Ratt every night, we became convinced that hairspray and lipstick were gonna be our ticket to massive success. Thank God we quickly came to our senses. I learned early on that trying to be part of what's fashionable is a bad move.

Jon in acoustic mode

If I'd started out looking like Boy George and ended up looking like Eddie Vedder, I'd have had some explaining to do!

'If you just wear a T-shirt and a pair of Levis and your record fails, at least you can go back to the bars knowing you never looked like your sister!'

Far from a return to the bars, Bon Jovi's fortunes continued to improve when they undertook their first headline tour of Britain. This included a successful slot at Donington's Monsters of Rock festival. By the mid-eighties, an appearance at Donington was considered the yardstick by which a band's success could be measured, and an invitation to perform was both an honour and a challenge. In 1985, Bon Jovi rose to this challenge with their customary gusto. They made the most of their tricky mid-afternoon billing to win over an initially cynical audience.

American audiences also gained an appreciation for the band's positive mentality when they performed at the televised charity concert Farm Aid, a spin off from the recent Live Aid spectacular. By the end of the tour, Bon Jovi had broken down the barriers, and had managed to shift over a million copies of their maligned second album. They nevertheless realised that their third album would have to sell more quickly if they were to hold on to their major label deal.

Slippery When Wet was recorded at Vancouver's Little Mountain Studios with Canadian producer Bruce Fairbairn. Bon Jovi knew they had to deliver – and deliver they most certainly did. It is not possible to clearly define just why *Slippery When Wet* exploded in such a momentous fashion. It goes without saying that the songs and production were utterly magnificent, and it goes without saying that Jon Bon Jovi's good looks and boy-next-door charm elevated him to sex symbol status. But for any album to sell as well as *Slippery*... there are obviously far more significant factors at work. Somehow, Bon Jovi's music tapped into the human spirit and refused to let go. It was part hard-rock bravado, and it was part honest human awareness. The wheels were set in motion, and a remarkable chain reaction took place. Whatever the cause, *Slippery*... has now come close to 18 million sales, making it the most successful hard rock album of all time.

From David Bryan's crashing keyboard extravaganza, which opened the album, to the lawless screams of last track, 'Wild in the Streets', this was a classic album from start to finish. Potent singles 'You Give Love a Bad Name' and 'Livin' on a Prayer', each with alluring, deadly hooks, both made it to Number One in America, and broke the band worldwide. The latter, with its lyrical dip into the lives of two ordinary Americans struggling to make ends meet, combined with the gritty personal drama of 'Wanted Dead Or Alive', began to affect people on an international level, and marked Bon Jovi out as a band to be cherished. People from all walks of life were turned on to what was, for most of them, a completely new band with a completely new sound. The floodgates had been opened.

'We were spaced out by the sudden success, man,' recalls Richie Sambora. 'We started getting served at the local pizza parlour a lot quicker! But when you live on the road, you soon take a kinda "interior" point of view. You only see the inside of places, usually hotels, and there's not much to remind you that you're in Germany or Japan or wherever.'

'Oh yeah,' nods Jon. 'I've woken up in hotel bedrooms thinking "Where the hell am I?" on quite a few occasions.'

'When you live on the road,' says Sambora, 'you learn to make every place you visit your home. It's either that or go crazy. It's all wrapped up with your mentality. You have to think of every place you visit as being a new home;

Somehow Bon Jovi's music tapped into the human spirit and refused to let go. It was part hard-rock bravado, and it was part honest human awareness.

hands on me Jon live

you try to associate something of that place with whatever means home to you. You learn to live out of a suitcase, and if you can't, you're in the wrong job!'

For Bon Jovi, 1986 and '87 passed by in a blur of touring and adulation. By now, they were the consummate live act, adding brilliantly timed pyrotechnics to their set, and even employing a remarkable stunt in which trick wires would lift Jon into the air, enabling him to 'fly' above the heads of the audience. The high-energy videos accompanying their hit singles emphasised the spectacular nature of their live shows.

Just two years after their original appearance, Bon Jovi were back at Donington, only this time as a headline act. They overcame physical exhaustion and dismal weather to deliver one of the festival's most legendary performances. Bon Jovi played a total of 140 shows in just sixteen months, appearing in all corners of the world. Jon, in particular, was a superstar, in demand everywhere he went. He returned to New Jersey a sick and exhausted man, and yet, somehow, was eager to throw himself once again into the cauldron of recording and touring.

Jon Bon Jovi

Bon Jovi's follow up album, titled *New Jersey* in tribute to their home state, promised more of the same, but was in fact more diverse in content. It was the work of a more mature band, who had developed and honed their art to perfection. The anthem 'Lay Your Hands On Me' was a glorious call to arms that opened proceedings, while the first single, 'Bad Medicine', was a cheeky rocker with a hint of Aerosmith, and 'Born To Be My Baby' was another earthy, blue-collar love song in the 'Livin' on a Prayer' tradition. The album also featured 'I'll Be There For You', a bluesy ballad that topped the American chart, and 'Blood On Blood', an emotional stampede that celebrated the value of friendship. Indeed, Bon Jovi themselves were beginning to see each other not merely as integral parts of a touring band, but as a brotherhood. It was with this spirit of unity that they yet again hit the long and winding road of touring. With the record selling millions, and single after single being released, the tour looked like it might never end.

In sixteen months, Bon Jovi circled the world three times and played 237 dates, a remarkable tally. They were the star attraction at the

Moscow Peace Festival, from which all proceeds went to the Make A Difference Foundation drugs awareness charity, and was by far the biggest event of its kind ever to have taken place in Russia. In a triumphant homecoming, they also fulfilled their childhood dreams by headlining Giants' Stadium in New Jersey.

'I remember telling everyone that if I could just headline Giants' Stadium, I would quite happily die afterwards!' says Jon, grinning broadly.

Ideally, Bon Jovi would have finished the tour there and then, but circumstances kept them on the road. Effectively, they had not had a break since the release of *Slippery When Wet*. By 1990, tensions were mounting. Their much-talked-about spirit of togetherness, strong though it was, was being subjected to pressure. Completely inaccurate press reports suggesting that Jon and Richie weren't speaking, and that Tico Torres had already quit persuaded Jon that the time had come to put the band on ice.

The group went their separate ways, with most outsiders assuming that the fairy tale had come to an acrimonious conclusion. In fact, the alleged split simply allowed the five band members the extended break they had not taken after the *Slippery...* tour. Jon, ever the workaholic, would have happily continued the grind, and instead immersed himself in writing and recording music for the film *Young Guns II – Blaze of Glory*, in which he had a cameo role. His endeavours surfaced in the form of a solo album, which sold in excess of two million copies, and spawned further hit singles.

Richie Sambora's simple love of music had not always tied in with Jon's ambitious work ethic. The guitarist now took things at a slower pace, recording his own album, *Stranger In This Town*, in 1991. Apart from the release from touring commitments, the album also gave Sambora the opportunity to pay homage to his blues and R&B roots. He was keen to experiment with certain styles that would never have been permissible within Bon Jovi. It was something Sambora needed to do, and *Stranger...*, warmly received by the critics, would certainly never be mistaken for a Bon Jovi album.

'We were lucky to come off the *New Jersey* tour with our minds and souls together,' recalls Jon. 'It was a very close call. When you've been on the road, away from home, in each other's company, tempers are bound to get frayed. I think it's testimony to the close relationship this band has that we came through to fight another day.

'The solo album was an important chapter for me, something for me to get out of my system. But, in a sense, Richie's solo record was even more important – he has a lot of blues influences in his playing which, I guess, he didn't feel were coming over real well in the context of what Bon Jovi does, so it was real important for him to express himself.'

David Bryan and Tico Torres both played on Sambora's record. Bryan also composed an instrumental soundtrack for the low budget horror film *Netherworld*, and Torres spent time building a boat and basking in anonymity. Regrettably, Alec John Such spent most of his time recovering from a motorcycle accident.

Bon Jovi on the 'New Jersey' tour

What was missing was the camaraderie and the sense of belonging, not to mention the unique chemistry that Jon and Richie's songwriting partnership had established. The time apart had allowed the band to mature as individuals, and had renewed the quintet's bond. By 1992, all five members were delighted to have the chance to return to their day jobs. They decided to start afresh, firing their long-time manager Doc McGhee, and handling their affairs themselves. *Keep the Faith*, Bon Jovi's comeback album, announced their return to the big time. It was not the eighties throwback album that many had expected. Instead, it proved that Bon Jovi now had all ten feet planted firmly in the nineties, embracing lyrics and influences that set them apart from almost anyone else on the scene.

In a society whose youth were besotted with the negativity of grunge, 'I Believe' and 'Keep the Faith' were powerful messages of hope. 'In These Arms' and 'I'll Sleep When I'm Dead' were typical, classic Bon Jovi songs, full of their usual stylistic traits, while 'Dry County' proved to be a staggering epic, a rich musical drama played out against a barren landscape of ruined industry and despair. It must rank as the finest, most involving song Bon Jovi have ever written. The group's renewed sense of brotherhood was made apparent by the cover art, a photograph of five hands linked together. As an album, *Keep the Faith* was not as immediate as its predecessors, but ultimately proved to be Bon Jovi's salvation. Their music was as real and affecting to people in the grunge-filled nineties as it had been in the eighties. Bon Jovi had reinvented themselves; a genuine master stroke.

'It was great that grunge came along,' says Jon of the movement that was supposed to bury him. 'It was the voice of a disillusioned generation. I couldn't write those kind of lyrics, but Kurt Cobain did a fine job. In the America that I grew up in, we were still falling for Ronald Reagan's nonsense, and believing that you could still get a well paid job and do better than your dad. Kids in the nineties are given nothing like these expectations. They're told they can't achieve this and they can forget about doing that. With that in mind, I think *Keep the Faith* has a really positive vibe.'

As a unit, Bon Jovi had also become more aware of their strengths and limitations. They knew only too well that their last tour had almost finished them. This time around, they resolved to play in the same number of countries, but with a more relaxed schedule which would allow them to take regular breaks. By this time, Jon himself had established

commitments beyond the group. In 1989, he had married his childhood sweetheart Dorothea Hurley, with whom he later had two children, Stephanie Rose and Jesse James. Jon is as fiercely proud of his wife and family as he is of his group and their achievements. His role as a full-time husband and father has brought a new sense of stability to his life. No longer does he feel the urge to pour every last drop of his energy into Bon Jovi. He has realised what Richie Sambora and the others knew all along – that there is life to be had outside the group.

For all that, Bon Jovi have remained one of the most prolific touring bands in the world, and have continued to rack up astronomical record sales. In 1994, they celebrated the tenth anniversary of their debut album with a greatest hits package, titled *Cross Road.* Complementing all the Bon Jovi favourites were two new songs, a spirited shuffle called 'Someday I'll Be Saturday Night' and a glossy, majestic ballad, 'Always'. Both were released as singles and both, unsurprisingly, were massive hits. 'Always', in particular, struck home, finishing 1994 as one of the year's biggest selling singles. To top it all, the band registered a festive hit with 'Please Come Home For Christmas', which was bolstered by a sexy video featuring supermodel Cindy Crawford. All proceeds of the single were allotted to charities, by no means the first or last time that Bon Jovi were to contribute to those less fortunate. Even during their two-year hiatus, they had managed to play a charity show in New Jersey on behalf of the homeless.

'I don't know why, but I felt the need to do something for kids that are handicapped and can't always look out for themselves,' explains Jon. 'When we came to a convenient break in our schedule, it seemed an ideal time to release a single for charity. And it turned out that Cindy Crawford was available and had agreed to be the love interest in the video. I said, "I get to kiss Cindy Crawford for seven hours? Fine!" '

Now that Bon Jovi were back on the world stage, nothing seemed beyond their grasp. Their 1995 album, *These Days,* was another ambitious and very diverse project which seemed to pick up where *Keep the Faith* had left off. It was a timely mixture of lustrous ballads, slick rockers and gritty epics. In the wake of 'Dry County', the title track probed such contemporary issues as unemployment and the demise of the American dream, while in contrast, 'Something for the Pain' was a sprightly rock 'n' roll song with a typically addictive chorus. Quickening its progress up the charts was an uncharacteristic video, in which the band poked gentle fun at 'serious' nineties stars like Pearl Jam's Eddie Vedder and Stone Temple Pilots' Scott Weiland. A number of star lookalikes were recruited, and were featured miming petulantly to the song's chorus. Some were outraged, but far more were amused. It was, if nothing else, a good laugh.

'It would be nice to think that we've never repeated ourselves due to artistic integrity,' ponders Jon, 'but the truth is that just as you change as a person, your musical tastes change, and so your writing has to change. It all comes with age and experience. The times when all I wanted to do was chase women are over. Now I've seen so many other things.

'There's a lot of inequality in American society that I can't alter and have had to come to terms with. I think that the latest album reflects that far more than any previous Bon Jovi album. I still think 'You Give Love a Bad Name' is a great song, but there's nothing remotely like that on *These Days*. I've got things on my mind now that didn't bother me in 1986, and I want to get them off my chest. Lyrically, it's way more introspective and the overall feel is a little darker."

Sadly, Bon Jovi had recorded *These Days* without the services of Alec John Such. The bassist, ten years Jon's senior and now well into his forties, had decided that enough was enough, and announced his departure. It was an amicable split, but a sad one bearing in mind that Bon Jovi had maintained the same line-up since the recording of their first album.

'Change is change and there's nothing you can do about it,' Jon shrugs. 'It was a major blow to lose one of the original members. We just had to accept it. We have nothing but the best to say about Alec, and I hope he's happy. Just because I want to constantly tour and make records doesn't mean that he should also feel that way. It's true that Alec started to leave this band a long time ago, but his commitment to recording was never under suspicion. If ever Bon Jovi get into the rock 'n' roll hall of fame, I hope Alec will be up there with us.'

Hugh McDonald, an experienced session musician and friend of Jon's, recorded all bass parts on *These Days*, and accompanied the band on tour. Strangely, McDonald is still primarily a session player and is rarely pictured with the group. Though unobtrusive on stage, he is indispensable to the band's sound.

The open air stadium shows that followed the release of *These Days* were the most successful and spectacular of the band's glittering career. Bon Jovi would perform for almost three hours, beginning in daylight and ending in darkness, accompanied by breathtaking pyrotechnics and aerial fireworks. At a time when most bands adhered to a minimalist policy of stripping everything down to basics, Bon Jovi remained one of a handful of bands willing to pull out all the stops to give their fans as much value for money as possible. All-day concerts, featuring three or four high-profile support acts, were now pretty much a Bon Jovi tradition.

Jon Bon Jovi

BON JOVI TRIVIA

Jon's mother, Carol, used to be a Playboy bunny girl. She bought Jon his first guitar and now helps to manage the official Bon Jovi fan club.

At High School, Jon appeared in a version of the stage musical *Mame*. He played Junior Babcock, a relatively minor role.

Keyboard player David Bryan was born on 7 February 1962 in Edison, New Jersey. He was classically trained at the renowed Juilliard School Of Music in New York.

Before joining Bon Jovi, drummer Tico Torres was managed by Bruce Ward – the same Bruce Ward that used to play Robin The Boy Wonder in the cult sixties TV show *Batman*.

Jon and Dorothea Bon Jovi own two identical red Ferrari sports cars, although Jon's day to day motor is a black Mercedes S500.

Jon's Underground Studios are so-called because that's exactly where they are – underground in his basement at home.

Current bass player Hugh McDonald actually played on the first ever Bon Jovi single, 'Runaway', as a session musician.

Richie Sambora is married to TV actress Heather Locklear. Tico Torres is married to Wonderbra girl Eva Herzigova.

Richie Sambora has been known to perform solo concerts at Hollywood's legendary House Of Blues.

When choosing songs to appear on *Slippery When Wet*, Bon Jovi recruited kids from the local pizza restaurant to help them decide. The team was named 'The Pizza Parlor Jury'.

In the days before Bon Jovi, Jon auditioned for the lead role in the film *Footloose* – but that was as far as he got. Richie, however, had a small role in the John Travolta movie *Staying Alive*. Unsurprisingly, he played a musician.

Richie Sambora

The sense of accomplishment and the challenge that exists for further accomplishment is cool

Jon Bon Jovi

In the midst of touring, Jon found time to star in a film, *The Leading Man*, following on from his role alongside Whoopi Goldberg in *Moonlight and Valentino*, and his all too brief appearance in *Young Guns II*. There is, however, no question of him abandoning Bon Jovi to pursue an acting career.

'It was just another outlet for me,' chuckles Jon, 'just something for me to do while I'm not making records. It's certainly not a means for me to quit my day job!'

Despite his ever increasing celebrity status, Jon has kept the faith in his band, his friends and his music. He has constantly paid tribute to the loyalty of his fans.

'These days, I don't just have the success of the band to be thankful for. I'm always extremely flattered that our fans care so much about the band. There are always people hanging out for us, and I haven't forgotten what it's like to be a fan. I don't find it threatening and I don't take it too seriously either. I have the stability of my family life and the fact that the band are all happy to fall back on. The sense of accomplishment and the challenge that exists for further accomplishment is cool.'

At Christmas in 1994, I was lucky enough to be invited to Jon's home in New Jersey. He lives within ten minutes of Richie Sambora's house, in the beautiful town of Rumson. That evening, as we drove through Rumson's frosty, festively lit streets, Jon pulled over to the kerb to marvel at a group of children and their parents singing carols around a Christmas tree. No one in that little group could have known that one of the world's biggest stars was in their midst. Jon remains as enchanted by people and their everyday lives as he was as a struggling musician in neighbouring Sayreville all those years ago. Through such a fascination Bon Jovi maintain a sense of warmth and hope with which they also paint the colours of their music. It is a warmth which allows their songs of friendship, faith and desire to appeal on a universal scale. It is the spirit of rock 'n' roll itself.

ALBUM DISCOGRAPHY:

Bon Jovi (1984)

7800 Degrees Fahrenheit (1985)

Slippery When Wet (1986)

New Jersey (1988)

Blaze of Glory - Young Guns II (Jon Bon Jovi) (1990)

Stranger In This Town (Richie Sambora) (1991)

Keep The Faith (1992)

Cross Road - The Best of Bon Jovi (1994)

These Days (1995)

Jon and Richie capture the spirit of rock'n'roll!

DEF LEPPARD

HEROISM

Heroism, calamity and glory. These are the three elements that seem to sum up the story of Def Leppard, a story more dramatic than any soap opera. Their rags to riches fairy tale, which has taken them from grimy Sheffield rehearsal rooms to the plateau of millionaire megastardom, has always been dogged by an element of tragedy. Though they have produced some of the most instantly recognisable music ever made, and have revelled in their success, an undercurrent of heartbreak has always been present. Somehow, Def Leppard have remained as dignified in crisis as they have in success. More importantly, they are one of the finest melodic rock acts ever to have drawn breath.

In May 1996, Def Leppard released their most recent album, *Slang*. It was the work of a satisfied band with a stable-line up, a band who no longer needed to worry about their profile. Although a few songs, notably the title track, were comparable with the lively party anthems of Leppard past, much of the album took a slightly darker, more introspective angle. The band – vocalist Joe Elliott, guitarists Phil Collen and Vivian Campbell, bassist Rick 'Sav' Savage, and drummer Rick Allen – now have a chance to look back at their astonishing career, and tie all the loose ends together.

The origins of Def Leppard can be traced back as far as Joe Elliott's school days. Even as a small child, the future frontman had amused his parents by screaming out the words to the Beatles' 'Love Me Do' while tearing about the house on stiff little legs. At school, the young Elliott applied his fertile imagination to designing concert posters and tickets for an imaginary rock band, Deaf Leopard!

'What happened,' says Joe, 'is that I got bored in art class. Instead of sitting around doing still life pictures of flowers and vases, I asked the teacher if I could design a poster for a rock show. I was really attracted by the glamour and power that rock music seemed to involve. I got into stuff like Bowie, T. Rex

CALAMITY AND GLORY

and Mott the Hoople. Of course, when I was designing posters for the fictitious band Deaf Leopard, the name was still spelt correctly. It was eventually our drummer who decided it would look better spelt phonetically, and we also noticed that it bore a vague resemblance to Led Zeppelin!'

Their story proper begins in 1978, when eighteen-year-old guitarist Steve Clark met another young guitar player, Pete Willis, at a Judas Priest gig in Sheffield. When it came together, the band, comprising Elliott, Sav, Clark and Willis, employed a succession of different drummers. For five youths in late seventies Sheffield, all the city had to offer was steel mills and dole queues. Everyone yearned to do something extraordinary, be it in sport, television or music. Anything to get out. It is not surprising that Leppard rehearsed with stoic devotion, often well into the small hours of the morning. This allowed them to develop into a cohesive unit, and gave them a chance to write songs together.

'It was only a matter of three or four weeks before I began to suspect that there was something of real note going down here,' remembers Joe. 'We rehearsed together with total dedication, firstly just bashing out covers. The first riff of our own that we came up with eventually turned into "Wasted". OK, so a lot of what we were doing back then was total shit, but it was all part of the learning process. But really, ever since Steve Clark had joined, I suspected that we could go places. Our earliest gigs were a combination of covers and our own material, and as time went on, we'd gradually add more of our own stuff.'

In 1979, a loan from Elliott's parents got the band on their way. They used the money to record the *Getcha Rocks Off* EP, which they released on their own Bludgeon Riffola label. They attempted to distribute the EP amongst local record shop owners. One of those approached, Peter Martin, was so impressed that he recommended the band to his friend, Frank Stuart-Brown, who had worked at WEA

'HAS THE LEPPARD CHANG ITS SPOTS?'

Vivian Campbell

Phil Collen

Rick Savage

Joe Elliot

Rick Allen

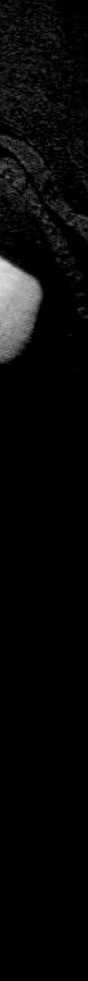

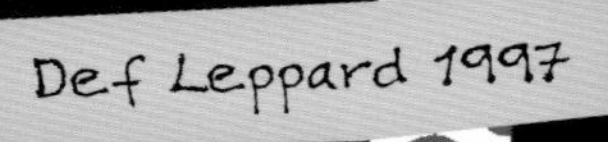
Def Leppard 1997

and Arista Records, and had contacts. The duo agreed to manage the band. At the same time, Leppard recruited fifteen-year-old Rick Allen as their permanent drummer. Through sheer hard work, their management created a storm of hype, convincing the media that Leppard were stars in the making.

Sounds critic Geoff Barton was particularly impressed, and ran a three-page article, proclaiming the arrival of the 'New Wave of British Heavy Metal'. Leppard were seen as the front runner of an important new movement. The record companies who had previously told them that metal was dead, and that punk was the way forward, were suddenly involved in a bidding war for their signatures. Phonogram emerged victorious, and immediately put the lads out on tour with the likes of Sammy Hagar and AC/DC.

'Peter Martin was a lovely, easy going bloke who genuinely liked the band and wanted to help,' says Joe, 'and Frank Stuart-Brown, initially at least, helped us to establish contacts at record companies. It's true that Geoff Barton was the first critic to latch on to us, but I had been plugging our band for what seemed like ages to the press before anything happened. I had absolutely inundated the people at *Sounds*. Back then, we were trying to compete with punk.'

Their debut album, *On Through the Night*, was released in 1980, and during the AC/DC tour, Leppard secured new, higher-powered management in the form of New Yorker Peter Mensch and his partner, Cliff Burnstein. Frank Stuart-Brown had felt that too much touring might lead to what he perceived as over exposure.

The band now had the opportunity to make their American debut, supporting Ted Nugent, an established American star. The British media, who liked to believe they had plucked Leppard from obscurity, now turned on the band, accusing them of 'selling out' to America, thereby 'abandoning' their loyal fans at home. The problem was compounded by the fact that Leppard had released 'Hello America' as a single. Even Geoff Barton, who had championed the band so enthusiastically in *Sounds*, posed the now famous question, 'Has the Leppard changed its spots?' as his cover line. They had, of course, done nothing of the sort, but during their slot at 1980's Reading Festival, legend has it that Leppard were almost driven off stage by former fans throwing rubbish at them.

'This is something that has been distorted by time,' counters Joe. 'The so-called backlash was nothing like as severe as it has been made out. I had

written the lyrics to "Hello America" long before any of this took off. It was just a song about a fantasy to go to California and enjoy the sun and sand. As for Reading, the main reason it was a difficult gig is because we had to follow Slade. In those days, it was traditional for kids at festivals to throw stuff. I don't think any more rubbish was thrown at us than at any of the other bands on the bill.

'Geoff Barton's comments about Leppard changing its spots were hurtful at the time, but he later apologised. You have to remember that we were one of the first bands Barton discovered. When he first came to Sheffield to see us, I met him at the station and we basically rolled out the carpet for him. Next time he came to see us, we weren't in a position to do that, and I guess he felt a bit snubbed, a little aggrieved.'

Like most bands in their position, Leppard knew that the second album would make or break them. They knew it had to be a solid, uncompromising rock album that would silence the critics. When the new record, *High 'n' Dry*, was released in 1981, enough humble pie was shoved down the media's throats to end all shouts of 'sell-out' forever. Bristling with energetic, aggressive tracks like 'Let It Go' and 'No No No', together with the tasteful, commercial rock of 'Bringin' On the Heartbreak', the album was hailed as a winner. In recording the album, Leppard had worked with respected producer Robert John 'Mutt' Lange. It was Lange's experience and expertise that allowed Leppard to develop the spacious, rounded sound and big harmonies for which they are now legendary.

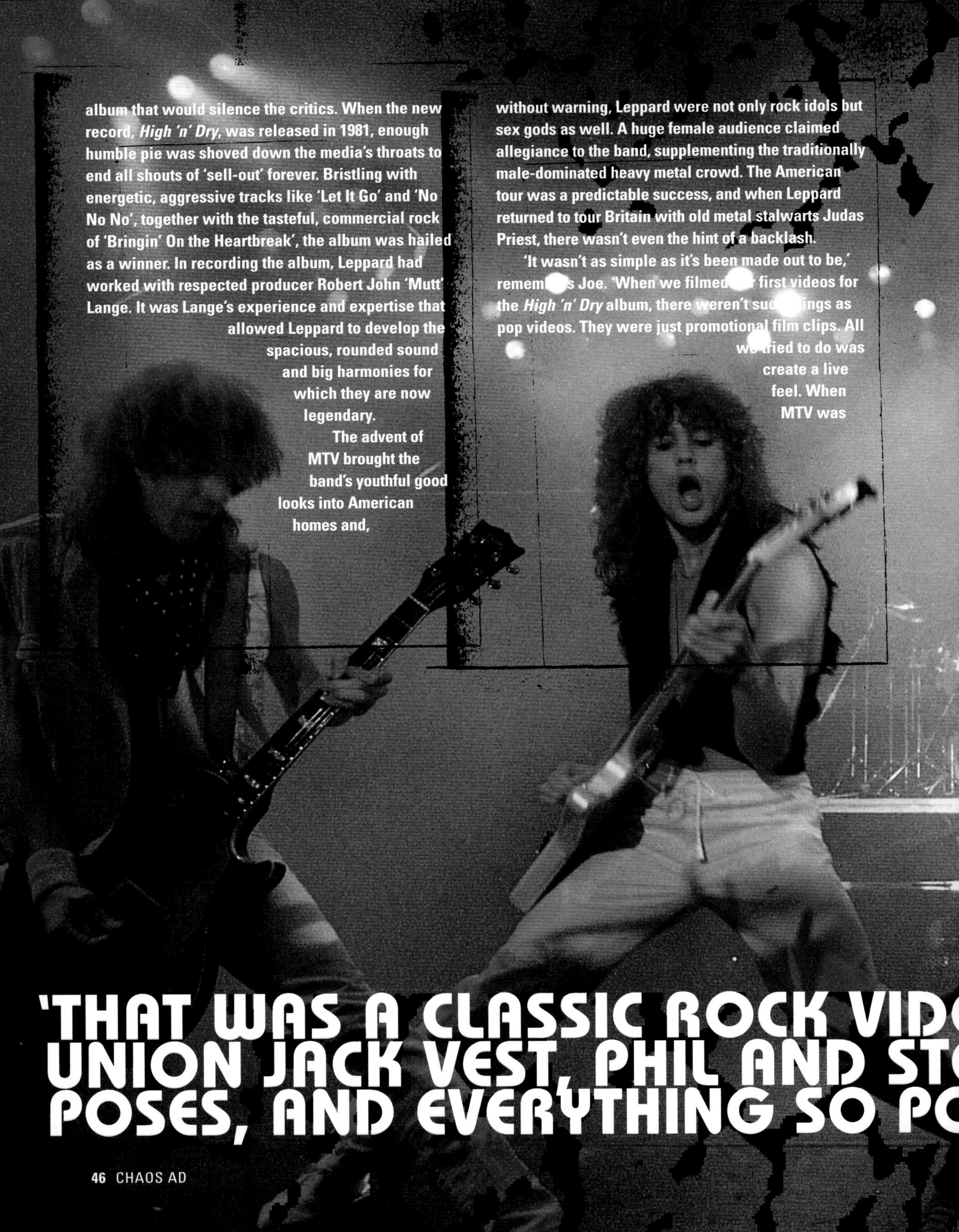

The advent of MTV brought the band's youthful good looks into American homes and, without warning, Leppard were not only rock idols but sex gods as well. A huge female audience claimed allegiance to the band, supplementing the traditionally male-dominated heavy metal crowd. The American tour was a predictable success, and when Leppard returned to tour Britain with old metal stalwarts Judas Priest, there wasn't even the hint of a backlash.

'It wasn't as simple as it's been made out to be,' remembers Joe. 'When we filmed our first videos for the *High 'n' Dry* album, there weren't such things as pop videos. They were just promotional film clips. All we tried to do was create a live feel. When MTV was

'THAT WAS A CLASSIC ROCK VID
UNION JACK VEST, PHIL AND ST
POSES, AND EVERYTHING SO PO

launched, the idea of making story or concept videos came along, but by then the album had been out for some time. By the time we were recording our third album, *Pyromania*, 'Bringin' On the Heartbreak' from *High 'n' Dry* was scaling the charts in America, mainly thanks to the video. That set us up nicely for *Pyromania*.'

With lasting fame at their fingertips, the band were determined not to loosen their grip. For *Pyromania*, they had again hooked up with Mutt Lange. Sadly, guitarist and founder member Pete Willis was finding it impossible to adjust to the breakneck schedule of Leppard's existence. With the mutual agreement of both parties, Willis left the band, and was replaced by ex-Girl

D, WITH ME IN MY
VE PULLING ALL THE ROCK STAR
WERFUL & VIBRANT'

guitarist Phil Collen. The Londoner was a seasoned and flamboyant performer, and no stranger to either stage or studio. He was the perfect addition to the ranks, and was soon turning his attention to the magnificent new riffs Steve Clark had written.

The recording of *Pyromania* was challenging for all, with Lange pushing each band member to their artistic limits. What eventually emerged in 1983, however, made all the tribulations seem worthwhile. *Pyromania* shifted the entire genre of hard rock into a different gear. It had three times more power and passion than anything Leppard had released before. The trademark vocal harmonies dug in like sharpened knives, while the guitar work of Messrs Clark and Collen simply pummelled the listener into a state of euphoria. On 'Photograph', Clark produced one of the greatest riffs of all time, while on 'Foolin'', 'Comin' Under Fire' and 'Rock of Ages', Leppard showed that they were amongst the best tunesmiths around. 'Die Hard the Hunter', meanwhile, developed an ambitious epic style, replete with warzone sound effects.

Pyromania blitzed the American charts, shifting millions of units, held off the top spot only by Michael Jackson's *Thriller*.

Rick Allen – triumph over tragedy.

A combination of stunning live shows and strong videos sent 'Photograph' into America's Top Ten. Leppard finished their U.S. tour with two sold-out dates at the Los Angeles Forum, playing to a total of 32,000 people.

'To be honest,' says Joe, 'we didn't see an improvement in our fortunes for quite some time. It was again a gradual process, and the video for "Photograph" had a lot to do with our success in America. Playing in Britain that time around was very disappointing. At Edinburgh we played to less than 200, and even in Sheffield the place was only half full. In Britain, "Photograph" only got to Number 41, but in America it was much bigger, mainly thanks to MTV. That was a classic rock video, with me in my Union Jack vest, Phil and Steve pulling all the rock star poses, and everything so powerful and vibrant.

'When we toured America, we ended up supporting Billy Squier. By the end of the tour it was becoming obvious that we were pulling in more punters than he was. In fact there was one gig in particular where we sold five times as many T-shirts!'

Leppard were well aware of the importance of their relationship with Mutt Lange, as vital to the development of their sound as George Martin had been to the Beatles. When Lange was unavailable to produce their fourth album, the band felt they were at a crossroads. Initially, they tried to record with Meat Loaf producer Jim Steinman, and then with Nigel Green, who had assisted with *High 'n' Dry*, but the recordings in both cases proved unsatisfactory. During a Christmas break in 1984, the already frustrating delay was dealt another, far more serious blow.

On New Year's Eve, Rick Allen was driving with his girlfriend on the A57 from Sheffield to visit his parents in Dronefield, Derbyshire. After an altercation with another driver, Allen rather foolishly pursued the other car at high speed. He suddenly lost control, the car skidding into a wall before

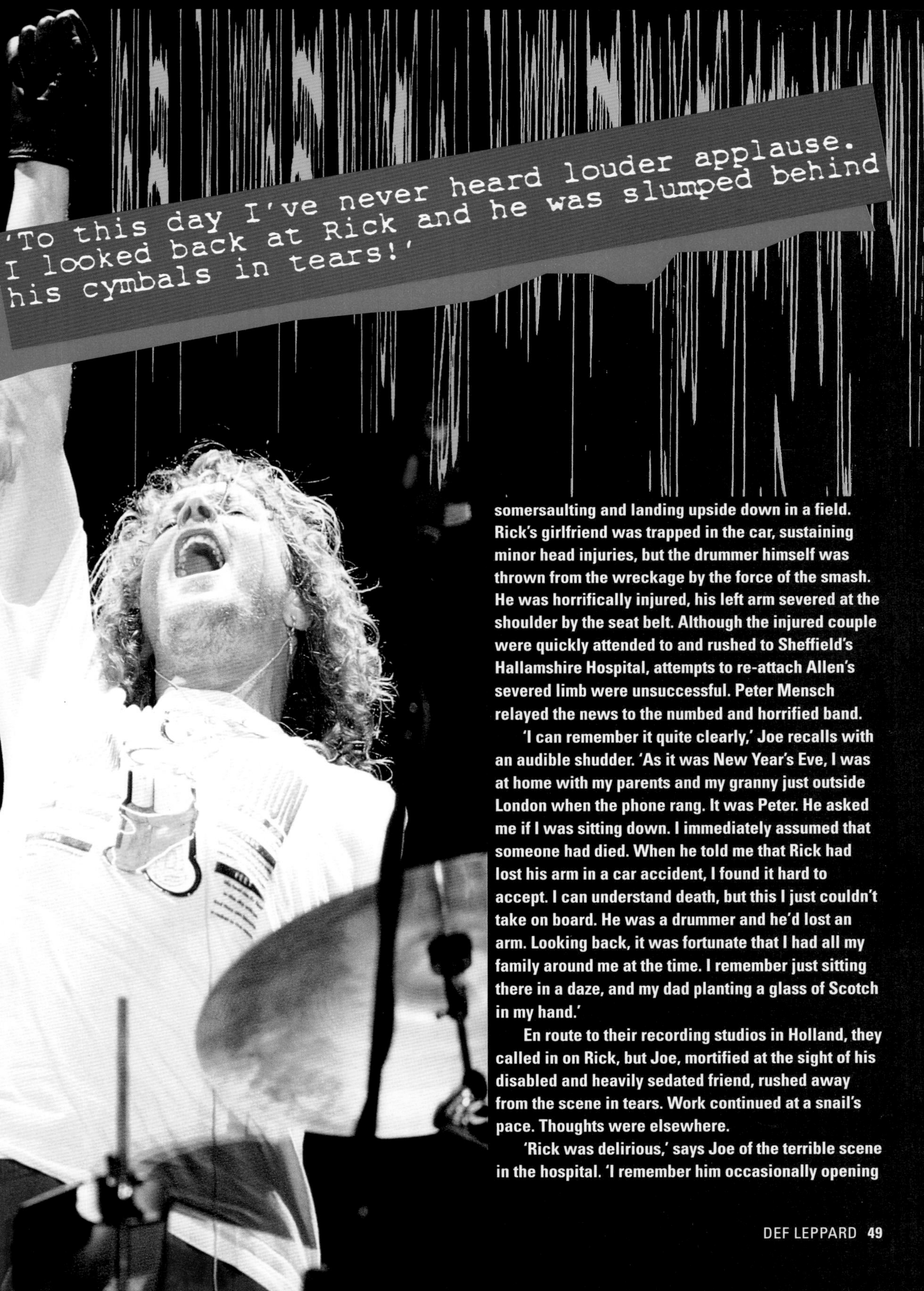

'To this day I've never heard louder applause. I looked back at Rick and he was slumped behind his cymbals in tears!'

somersaulting and landing upside down in a field. Rick's girlfriend was trapped in the car, sustaining minor head injuries, but the drummer himself was thrown from the wreckage by the force of the smash. He was horrifically injured, his left arm severed at the shoulder by the seat belt. Although the injured couple were quickly attended to and rushed to Sheffield's Hallamshire Hospital, attempts to re-attach Allen's severed limb were unsuccessful. Peter Mensch relayed the news to the numbed and horrified band.

'I can remember it quite clearly,' Joe recalls with an audible shudder. 'As it was New Year's Eve, I was at home with my parents and my granny just outside London when the phone rang. It was Peter. He asked me if I was sitting down. I immediately assumed that someone had died. When he told me that Rick had lost his arm in a car accident, I found it hard to accept. I can understand death, but this I just couldn't take on board. He was a drummer and he'd lost an arm. Looking back, it was fortunate that I had all my family around me at the time. I remember just sitting there in a daze, and my dad planting a glass of Scotch in my hand.'

En route to their recording studios in Holland, they called in on Rick, but Joe, mortified at the sight of his disabled and heavily sedated friend, rushed away from the scene in tears. Work continued at a snail's pace. Thoughts were elsewhere.

'Rick was delirious,' says Joe of the terrible scene in the hospital. 'I remember him occasionally opening his eyes and looking at us as if he had gone insane and wanted to kill us. What made it worse was all the press vultures hanging around outside. One of them even stole a doctor's uniform in an attempt to get in and take pictures.'

What happened next remains one of the most remarkable chapters in rock history. Rather than succumbing to the obvious idea that he would never play drums again, Allen investigated the possibilities of having a prototype drum kit built which would allow him to use his feet to play everything he had once played with his left arm. The kit was designed, built and delivered. With the goal of continuing his career with Def Leppard, Allen applied himself to the gargantuan task ahead with amazing fortitude. Endless modifications needed to be made to the kit, and Allen's complete rehabilitation was to take two years. Rick was nevertheless to return to the studio.

With the sudden availability of Mutt Lange, the band decided to start the recording procedure again from scratch. As arduous as the process seemed, they knew they had to aim for perfection. After *Pyromania*, and their lengthy absence from the scene, nothing else would do. To bypass the boredom, and remind fans that the band still existed, Peter Mensch booked them to appear at the legendary Donington Monsters of Rock festival in 1986. Having not played to a major audience for years, Def Leppard faced the prospect of entertaining a crowd of 70,000. The band did not shrink from the task, delivering an electrifying set to rapturous response. A poignant moment arrived when Rick Allen was introduced, and was reduced to tears by the ovation he received. Def Leppard were back.

'We had warmed up for Donington with a few very low-key dates in Ireland. Jeff Rich, Status Quo's drummer, helped us out. We'd have two drum kits on stage, one of which Jeff would play. However, when we played in Ballybunion, Jeff couldn't make it on time and Rick played forty-five minutes on his own. After the next gig, Jeff looked at Rick and said "Well, I guess you don't need me any more."

'Donington was remarkable. I wasn't intending on introducing Rick and making a big deal over it, but I sensed the crowd wanted me to. When I said, "Ladies and gentlemen, Rick Allen", the noise was deafening, like the loudest hair dryer you can imagine. To this day I've never heard louder applause. I looked back at Rick and he was slumped behind his cymbals in tears!'

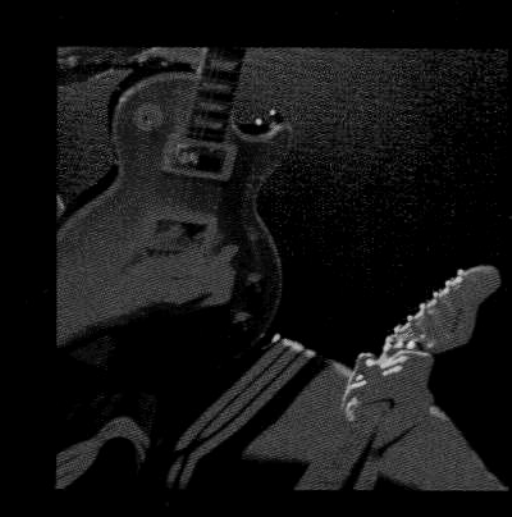

Riding the crest of this wave, they spent another year recording, finally presenting the fruits of their long labour to an audience ravenous for new Leppard material. This was *Hysteria*, and, like its predecessor, it soon came to be regarded as one of the greatest rock albums ever made. Rousing rock anthems like 'Pour Some Sugar On Me' and 'Armageddon It', both destined for Top Five status in

ALBUM DISCOGRAPHY:

Getcha Rocks Off (EP) (1979)
On Through the Night (1980)
High 'n' Dry (1981)
Pyromania (1983)
Hysteria (1987)
Adrenalize (1992)
Retro Active (1993)
Vault - Greatest Hits 1980-1995 (1995)
Slang (1996)

LET'S GET ROCKED

Phil and Vivian live and

America, were interspersed with gorgeously executed ballads, including 'Love Bites' and the title track. In terms of songwriting this album was second to none, and in terms of production, it was years ahead of its time. It hit the top spot on both sides of the Atlantic, eventually selling a monumental fifteen million copies. *Kerrang!* journalist Alison Joy hailed it as the album of the decade.

'Making and finishing that album was hell, quite frankly,' admits Joe. 'It took so long and cost so much. Some people thought we'd never finish it, and others thought we'd never recoup. We needed to sell four million copies just to break even, but incredibly, we pulled it off and went far beyond that. We knew that we would stand or fall on this album, and we had a producer who had staked his reputation on it. It's easily the most ambitious studio project we were ever involved with.'

Leppard embarked on a mammoth, 227-date, fourteen month world tour to promote *Hysteria*. Their bigger shows in America were performed 'in the round', i.e. with a circular stage in the middle of the arena rather than at one end, allowing audiences to be nearer the band, and also increasing the available seating capacity. The tour ended in October 1988 at the Memorial Arena in Seattle. Exhausted, Def Leppard returned to their respective homes knowing they were five of the richest and most famous young men in the business of music.

Sadly, their happiness was marred by a shadow that grew ever larger and more ominous as soon as the tour ended. Over the next two years, as Leppard prepared for their next album, the shadow was turning into a darkness that threatened to consume them. For everyone in the band it was plain to see that Steve Clark's increasing reliance on alcohol was destroying him. They went to desperate measures to curb their friend's addiction, but were unable to save him. Clark went to and from rehabilitation clinics again and again, but to no avail. Like many rock stars, he was not equipped to handle fame at the highest level, consistently drinking himself to oblivion when the routine of touring was removed and fatally, refusing to accept the severity of his problem.

'For Steve, the problem had always been there, and fame, and the opportunity to get drunk more often just made it worse,' Joe explains. 'I had seen Steve coughing up blood when he was a teenager, so the problem itself was nothing new. I think it's important to note that Steve was never irresponsible about his role in the group. He would never drink before going on stage. When we came off tour, Steve had more and more time to indulge his addiction. Not many people understand that Steve was literally addicted. He was physically unable to fight it, and unable to stop. Whereas most people's bodies are geared to fight the effects of alcohol, Steve literally could not resist. It wasn't a question of willpower, it was physical.'

Steve Clark was found dead at his flat in Chelsea on 8 January 1991. He had consumed a lethal cocktail of alcohol and painkillers. Def Leppard were deeply upset at the loss of their friend, but sadly, not shocked. During the last months of Steve's life, each member of the band had silently known that it was no longer a question of if Steve would die, but when. Clark, a shy and humble character, was one of the greatest riff-mongers of his generation, the epitome of a rock guitarist in every sense. Leppard, somehow, had to continue without him.

'It was obviously a traumatic time, waiting to record *Adrenalize*, and knowing that Steve was in no fit state to join us,' says Joe. 'By the time of his death, we already had seven songs written, and we decided to press on with just the four of us. We wrote "White Lightning" as a tribute to Steve. It was a relief to get those feelings out in the open. In a sense, "Let's Get Rocked", which we wrote after that, was the complete opposite, and was almost an exorcism of those negative feelings. To be honest, I'm thirty-six now, and it's hard to relate to the lyrics in that particular song!'

Phil Collen performed all guitar parts on Adrenalize following the tragic death of Steve Clark.

The band had once again demonstrated their legendary persistence in the face of adversity. In the absence of not only Clark, but Lange, who was busy producing Bryan Adams' latest album, they worked with producer Mike Shipley, finally delivering *Adrenalize* in 1992. It was a remarkable return, a surprisingly upbeat selection of songs, with harder guitars and playful, tongue-in-cheek lyrics. It was another multi-million seller, an astounding feat in the grunge-dominated nineties, at a time when most melodic rock acts were struggling to hang on to their record deals, never mind sell out arenas. With hit singles like 'Let's Get Rocked' and 'Heaven Is', Leppard were striving to restore brightness and fun to a despondent rock scene. And succeeding.

'White Lightning', however, took a dramatically different direction. In a poignant seven-minute epic, the band offered a thought-provoking insight into the mind of the addict. It took no feat of imagination to picture Steve Clark as a prisoner caught in the vicious circle of needing and not knowing how to stop. Never before had Def Leppard written lyrics as personal as this, a fact that made the song all the more moving. The band again toured the world, this time playing a mind-boggling 241 dates. Joe would introduce 'White Lightning' by blowing a kiss towards heaven.

By this time, of course, Leppard had recruited Irishman Vivian Campbell to complete their line-up.

Campbell had already played in such bands as Whitesnake and Dio, and was known not only for his superb musicianship, but for his solid and stable personality. He nevertheless had to defeat several other contenders for the much sought-after position. Although Campbell is relatively new to the ranks, his influence should not be understated. He has effectively settled a traumatised band who had lost both original guitarists, one tragically, and whose drummer had only been able to continue through his own remarkable strength of character.

'That was the happiest time of all for the band, at least up until now,' beams Joe. 'From a professional point of view, the band was incredibly tight, and we were playing the best shows of our lives. There was obviously a lot of work to be done, because it had been so long since *Hysteria*, but we were well aware by this time that things don't happen overnight. At a time when bands like Nirvana and Stone Temple Pilots were really happening, it felt great to know we were selling more records than both those bands.

Joe Elliott

'From a personal point of view, I've never been able to sing so well for so long. I've always suffered on-going problems with my throat, possibly because I abused my voice so much when I was younger. This time round, things were more consistent. And Phil, who in his drinking days with Steve was known as one of the Terror Twins, cut out alcohol for good. He hasn't touched a drop for years.'

Def Leppard were superstars. In 1993, they made an emotional return to Sheffield, headlining a four-band bill at the city's Don Valley Stadium. Shortly afterwards, they issued *Retro Active*, a collection of re-recorded out-takes that had never made it onto previous albums. A few tracks allowed Campbell to make his recording debut with the band, while others featured Clark's original contributions.

As a period of rest and inactivity again beckoned, Leppard plugged the gap by releasing *Vault*, a greatest hits album, from which an exclusive track, 'When Love and Hate Collide', was released as a single to become their biggest UK hit to date. A few months later, an entirely new album, *Slang*, hit the shops, producing yet more hit singles and tour dates. It was produced by Pete Woodroffe; Leppard had finally cast off Mutt Lange's mantle, dismissing ideas that they were unable to operate without him. Recording *Slang* was easily the most fun Joe has ever had making an album.

'It was approached completely differently to anything else we'd done,' he states. 'More importantly, it was the first album we'd ever done where we knew exactly what we wanted it to sound like. On other records, we'd gone into the studio not quite knowing what we'd end up with. We were all in total agreement, and knew exactly where we were headed. It couldn't have been much more different to *Hysteria*. This time we didn't want a huge, ballistic drum sound, and we didn't want computers affecting every facet of the sound. We wanted it to be much more raw and stripped down.

'It felt great to be a rock 'n' roll group again. Most of the songs are just slightly improved versions of the original demos. In fact, "Deliver Me" was more or less recorded in one take, and the original lead vocal on "Slang" was recorded in my bedroom. We weren't exactly a garage band, but we were certainly no more than a villa band!

'Touring is more fun than ever right now,' he continues. 'We've done away with fancy gadgetry like rotating drum risers. Like the album, it's a stripped down, basic rock 'n' roll show; just us and a huge bank of Marshalls. We're aware that the album isn't doing as well as some of our previous records, but we're still selling out 12,000-seat arenas and that to me is good business. This is undoubtedly the most enjoyable chapter in our career.'

Def Leppard are in the enviable position of having nothing left to prove. They have already exceeded their wildest teenage dreams, and have sold in excess of forty million albums. Conquering the world has come at enormous personal expense, but for all the tragedy and trauma, they have always returned from the brink of oblivion stronger and more versatile than before. With the faith and fraternity of soldiers returning from war, they will continue to fly the flag.

JOE ELLIOTT

Favourite album: Ziggy Stardust by David Bowie. It came out in 1972.

First gig attended: T. Rex in Sheffield.

Definition of success: Success happens when you achieve a state of happiness.

Most embarrassing tour story: I was once wearing very tight trousers at the time when it was fashionable to do so, and I managed to split them open very embarrassingly seconds before going on stage.

Most ridiculous thing a fan has done: There was this girl who wrote down the words 'I love Joe Elliott' 250,000 times!

Favourite food: Japanese.

Causes supported: Cancer research.

What would surprise someone most about you? Early on in our career, we supported the Human League. We've also played with the Nolan Sisters.

If your house was burning, what would you save first? Definitely my CD collection!

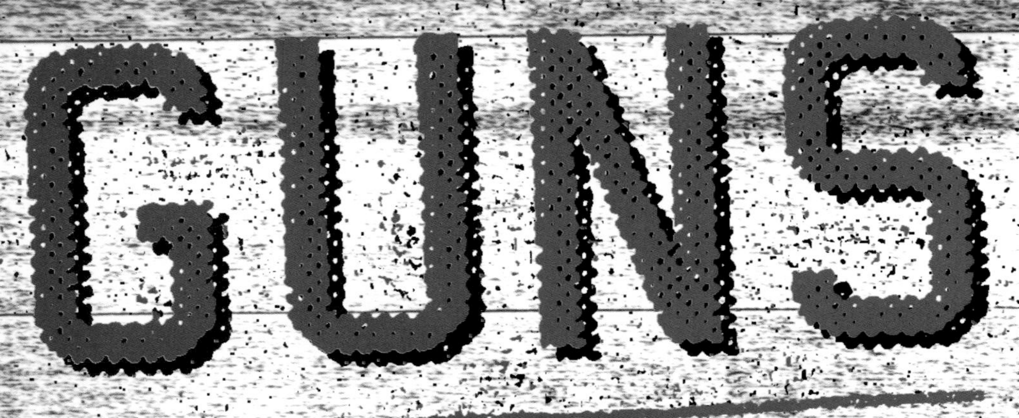

Easter Monday, 20 April 1992. The occasion was the Freddie Mercury Tribute Concert For AIDS Awareness at London's Wembley Stadium. For many, fans and pundits alike, this was Guns N'Roses' finest moment.

However, right up until the gates opened at Wembley that day, gay rights activists, justifiably outraged by the song 'One In A Million' which berates 'faggots' for spreading 'some fucking disease', had campaigned to have Guns N'Roses removed from the bill, and threatened to disrupt the band's performance should it go ahead. They argued that the Gunners' appearance at an event supposedly intended to celebrate the life of the famously bisexual Mercury *and* highlight the universal, non-selective threat of AIDS was entirely inappropriate.

The classic original line-up

On the day, though, there were no incidents. Guns N'Roses, and most critically Axl, carried themselves with dignity, and the friction that was expected to be created by the proximity of so many fragile egos never materialised. In something like thirty minutes of total stage time Guns N'Roses almost managed to wipe away five years of scandalous headlines, outrageous lyrics and excessive hedonism. More importantly, the band appeared to have won the approval not only of Queen, but also of Elton John, himself openly bisexual, and so laid to rest any suspicion that the Guns camp was a hotbed of homophobic paranoia.

ROSES

Rewind to 1985 and two pals, Jeff Isbell and Bill Bailey, who had traded in the uncertain pleasures of Lafayette, Indiana for the dubious delights of Hollywood, California. Izzy Stradlin and W. Axl Rose, as they preferred to be known, had come West with the express intention of putting together the ultimate rock 'n' roll band.

Axl, Izzy had decided, with his wildman looks and unpredictable nature, would make the perfect frontman, and the pair proceeded to assemble a suitable line-up. Eventually guitarist Tracii Guns (who would later form LA Guns), drummer Rob Gardner, and a bass-playing native of Seattle named Michael 'Duff' McKagan were recruited, and after operating as Rose, and Hollywood Rose, the fledgling superstars finally adopted the name Guns N'Roses. Their first mini-tour, christened the 'Hell Tour', was a modest enough affair, but Gardner and Tracii Guns were unwilling to hit the highway at that stage. They both pulled out at the last minute.

It was now that Duff threw in the names of the guitar player and drummer from a band called Road Crew that he had hooked up with when he first arrived in California. The pair, Slash (born Saul Hudson in Stoke-on-Trent, England) and Steven Adler (born in Cleveland, Ohio) hadn't impressed McKagan, but they were available, Guns N'Roses were desperate, and so Izzy was dispatched to seek them out. Slash remembers their first encounter vividly.

'I was working in a guitar store at the time, and I'd done this drawing of Aerosmith that somebody had printed up. Izzy came into the store and asked if I had a copy, and in the course of the conversation he mentioned that he had a band going. Anyway, he came over to my place after I got off work and played

me a tape that had this tiny little screaming voice in the background. I went to see them play at this place called Gazzari's, and my first impression was, okay, I just wanna steal the singer. Straight away I thought Axl was a really dynamic frontman, but at the time I just didn't think Izzy could play guitar. Anyway, they kind of came as a pair, and Izzy and I developed a complementary style really quickly.'

The band's building reputation as a feral live happening earned them an enviable deal with Geffen Records.

'You know rock music is always changing,' offers Slash when required to ponder what it was about Guns N'Roses that made them stand out from the literally hundreds of wannabe bands that made up the Hollywood pack. 'It goes through these surges of really creative, brilliant stuff, and then drops into these absolute lows when it almost seems like it's dead. We came along, doing stuff like nobody else was doing, at a time when music was at one of those low points. I guess it was almost like a fluke really, but we seemed to touch a nerve with everybody.'

After securing management for its latest signing, Geffen decided to put Guns N'Roses straight into the studio. The man chosen to record the band's particular brand of sonic frenzy was the relatively unknown Mike Clink. Fruitless attempts were made to hire multi-million selling engineer Spencer Proffer, and legendary Kiss frontman Paul Stanley was turned down after he had offered to rewrite some of the Gunners' material.

Establishing a pattern that was to repeat itself five years later, progress in the studio was at first fitful, hardly helped by a bucketful of Geffen cash which Izzy, Slash and Steven in particular blew on drugs. Doubtless worried about their investment, Geffen were determined to get something in the stores with the band's name on it as quickly as possible, and the limited edition EP *Live ?!*@ Like a Suicide* was hastily put together. The EP included two cover versions, 'Nice Boys' by legendary Australian brawlers Rose Tattoo, and Aerosmith's 'Mama Kin', as well as a brace of original tunes, 'Move to the City' and 'Reckless Life', which rather neatly summed up the band's buccaneering lifestyle. The record was a huge success, quickly selling out all 10,000 copies and creating a useful media stir in advance of the album proper.

Following a hectic promotional trip to London, which took in three shows at Soho's Marquee club, Guns N'Roses' debut album *Appetite For Destruction* was finally released in August 1987, and the world's rock literati tied themselves

Gilby Clarke
Slash
Slash

Axl Rose

in knots looking for adequate superlatives to describe it. The perfect antidote to the somewhat predictable eighties, it was immediately hailed as the most significant album of the decade. It took the disparate tastes of the five members and melded them into a viciously primitive amalgam of metal, punk, and swaggeringly good rock 'n' roll. Here

was Guns N'Roses' stall laid out for all to see: the lifestyle ('It's So Easy', 'Anything Goes'), the vices ('Mr Brownstone, 'Nightrain'), the loves ('Sweet Child o' Mine'), and the aspirations ('Paradise City') of the most incendiary new rock band in the world.

Typically, the record-buying public remained unmoved, and it was to take a year of grinding roadwork and several videos adored by MTV before the record was to reach the Number One spot on the U.S. *Billboard* album chart and really start to sell by the million.

'I never really gave a shit about success,' recalls Slash. 'And when it did happen it took me totally by surprise. We'd been on the road for a whole year and we only knew that the album was doing well when the crowd response started to get massive. The record company used to call us up and tell us what number it went to in the chart and how many copies we sold but I didn't really appreciate what it all meant until we got dropped off at the airport after one tour and I got asked for an autograph in a liquor store.'

As well as fame and fortune, *Appetite...* also handed Guns N'Roses their first major controversy. It was the record's sleeve, apparently depicting a rape scene, that caused the trouble. Several chainstores refused to stock it. To this day Slash remains unmoved by the hubbub.

'You know, at that particular time Tipper Gore [wife of then senator Al Gore and vociferous campaigner against 'offensive' lyrics and images on rock records] was enjoying her heyday, so the fuss over the sleeve didn't really surprise me at all. Anyway, life's too short to worry about that kind of shit. Guns N'Roses is always gonna be the kind of band that's gonna do whatever it's gonna do regardless. And you know what? Without all the conflict and the controversy, things wouldn't be half as interesting.'

One controversial incident that the band most assuredly did not savour occurred when they appeared at the annual Monsters of Rock Festival at Castle Donington in 1988. An over-excited crowd and slippery ground conditions combined to create a perilous situation in front of the stage which Guns N'Roses were only too aware of. The band did everything in its power to calm things down but all to no avail. Two fans, Alan Dick and Landon Siggers, had already lost their lives in the crush. Predictably, the English tabloids practically blamed the band for the tragedy, completely ignoring Axl's frantic attempts to alleviate the situation.

...N' Roses is always gonna be the kind of band that's gonna do whatever it's gonna do regardless. And you know what? Without all the conflict and the controversy, things wouldn't be half as interesting.

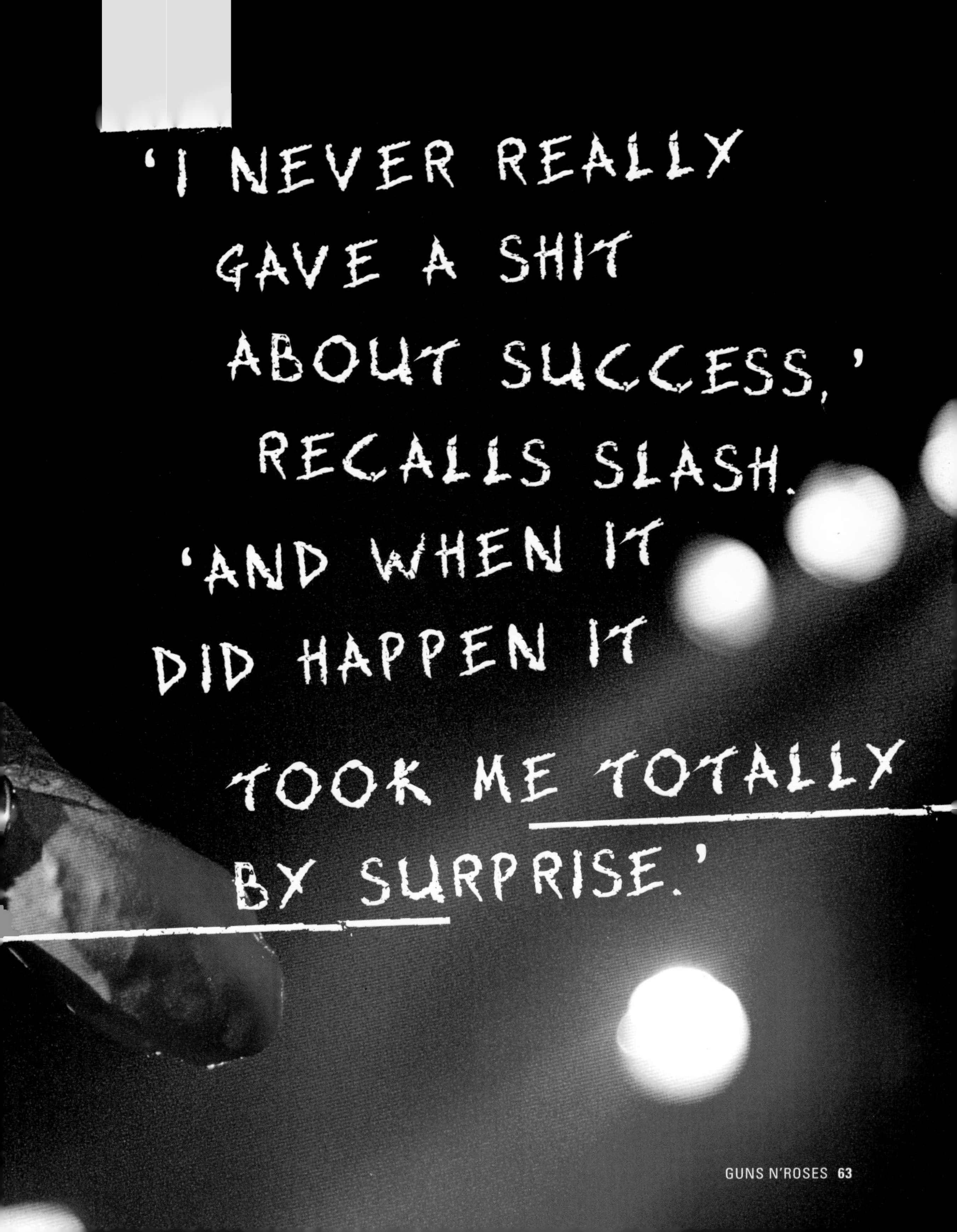

'I NEVER REALLY GAVE A SHIT ABOUT SUCCESS,' RECALLS SLASH. 'AND WHEN IT DID HAPPEN IT TOOK ME TOTALLY BY SURPRISE.'

'Oh well, they always do that,' reflects Slash ruefully. 'Press is press, you know. They take something that happens and twist it into something that's gonna sell newspapers. We happened to be the bad boy group at the time, and they just had a ball with us. We didn't actually find out that anybody had died until we got back to our hotel and it was a huge shock. You don't necessarily feel *responsible* when something like that happens, but just being there when it did was enough to bring down a serious black cloud on us all.'

Back home in the U.S., Geffen had decided to draw a line under 1988, a year of both triumph and tragedy for the Gunners, by responding to huge public demand and re-releasing the *Live ?!*@ Like a Suicide* EP backed with four acoustic leftovers from the *Appetite...* sessions. The package, in a mocking lampoon of the increasingly sensationalist way the band's activities were being reported, was titled *GN'R LIES – the Sex, the Drugs, the Violence, the Shocking Truth*, and it came wrapped in a sleeve laid out to resemble the front page of a particularly tacky tabloid rag. Of course, one of the acoustic numbers was the infamous 'One In A Million', which as well as upsetting the gay community, created outrage over Axl's use of the word 'niggers' – a gaffe which must have been particularly hurtful to the half-black Slash. Axl apologised, but it still remains an issue.

'Let's just say that I didn't approve of that song at all, and I refuse to play it live,' Slash says. 'It's still a really touchy subject.'

As if to escape the heat, Guns N'Roses headed off for their first dates in Australia at the end of 1988. It was a visit enlivened no end by the unceremonious removal of support band Kings of the Sun from the tour, and Axl narrowly escaping arrest in Sydney after apparently endorsing the use of drugs from the stage. Business as usual, then.

Most of 1989 was spent enjoying well-deserved multi-platinum success, and yet becoming so distanced from each other that an absolute split was at one point a genuine possibility. Motivated by boredom, Slash, Izzy and Steven had slipped further into the murky world of chemical abuse, and the logistical effort required to get all five members of the group into a studio proved too great to achieve. A drastic wake-up call was needed, and it was Slash who picked up the phone, booking the band to support the Rolling Stones across four nights in October at the massive LA Coliseum.

'My way of dealing with things when there's a discrepancy in the band and we're not working because of it is to find some vehicle to put us in a working situation. So when those Stones gigs were offered to us I accepted with open arms, and it worked – the band literally got back together over those four nights.'

Not that this would be the impression gained by anyone who witnessed Axl threatening to resign live on stage at the first of the four shows if 'certain members' of Guns N'Roses didn't clean up their drug-addled act.

'Yeah, I was strung out at the time,' Slash admits. 'And after the first show we were on the verge of breaking up. By the third and fourth shows, though, things got worked out and we started to make amends. That's why I wanted to do those shows in the first place. I knew that would happen.'

The first result of Guns N'Roses' newly regained work ethic was the ambitious, epic 'Civil War', the first Guns tune to feature newly recruited keyboard player Dizzy Reed. Carrying a thoughtfully emotive lyric concerning the futility of warfare, it utterly confounded all those who had the band pegged as airhead rock bozos. It was debuted live at the yearly Farm Aid benefit show in Indiana. This was to be Steven Adler's last concert with Guns N'Roses.

The hapless drummer had been by no means the sole member of the band to have flirted with chemical disaster, but he had been singularly unable to control his habits enough to let serious work on the second album get under way. After repeated warnings, Adler was fired. It was an outcome that caused Slash particular regret: he and Adler had been school friends, and indeed, it had been Steven that had persuaded the teenage Slash to take up the guitar.

'The situation with Steven really was irretrievable. We tried so many things to straighten him out. The rest of us basically went through the same thing and came out the other side, but Steven couldn't differentiate between getting really high all the time, and being able to play. When you get so fucked up that you can't see things in their proper perspective, then you're screwed.'

Axl on stage at the Freddie Mercury tribute concert in London

After replacing Adler with former Cult drummer Matt Sorum, Guns N'Roses were finally able to begin work on their second real album by the end of 1990, taking time out only to headline two nights at the massive Rock In Rio II festival. The shows went well, especially for the two newcomers who amply justified their appointment in front of an insane crowd of 125,000. As usual though, it was the offstage activities of the band that caught the headlines. Axl was reputedly isolating himself more and more from the rest, and a small army of heavies – hired to shield Guns from contact with the outside world – gleefully beat up anyone who tried to sneak an unauthorised photo.

Another addition to the guitarist s tattoo collection

SLASH

Favourite album: Rocks by Aerosmith.

First gig attended: Aerosmith with AC/DC in 1977.

Most embarrassing tour story: There are just too many, but most involve me being drunk.

Favourite food: Just spaghetti and meat balls.

Hobbies: I'm an avid collector of toy dinosaurs. And of course, there's the snakes. I guess I have over three hundred now!

Causes supported: Charities concerning children: disease research and help for the homeless.

What would surprise someone most about you? That I'm actually a little bit articulate and very hard working.

If your house was burning, what would you save first? If you don't count my wife, I'd have to get my cats out. I have twelve of them.

Following the Rio jaunt, work continued on the album, now known to be titled *Use Your Illusion*. Mike Clink had again been hired to oversee the project ('he's like the fifth Beatle, or something'), with Sex Pistols producer Bill Price drafted in for the final mix. As a result of eleventh-hour alterations and Axl's insistence on new material being added, the album's projected spring release came and went, and in all there were to be a further *ten* abandoned release dates across the summer of 1991 before the mammoth *Use Your Illusion* package finally hit the shops in September: thirty songs in all, spread across two double-length albums, *Use Your Illusion* volumes I and II. Two and a half hours of music.

'We basically tapped ourselves out on that one,' says Slash, demonstrating a little-known talent for understatement. 'We had a certain amount of new material, some old songs like "Don't Cry" and "You Could Be Mine", and of course, the covers [Dylan's 'Knockin' On Heaven's Door' and Wings' 'Live And Let Die']. Whatever you think of them, those two albums are totally indicative of the way the band was feeling at the time. Letting all that stuff out and releasing all the frustration of the previous year was like an orgasm. We basically got a lot of stuff out of our system and wiped the slate clean.'

The twin albums instantaneously installed themselves in the top two chart positions on both sides of the Atlantic, with American advance orders alone numbering an astonishing four million. Critical reaction was more measured. Nobody denied that the records had plentiful moments of sheer genius (the blustering 'You Could Be Mine'; the poppy, psychedelic 'The Garden'; the darkly compelling 'Coma'), but some observers commented that the Gunners' quality control mechanism was kaput, and that 'Live And Let Die' and Axl's piano led ballads 'November Rain' and 'Estranged' were pompously inflated.

Slash concedes, 'If it had been just up to me personally, I would have done a simple record like *Appetite...*, but if you want to be conscientious about being part of a band then you have to compromise.'

A world tour in support of the *...Illusion* records had already kicked off back in May. It would see Guns N'Roses circling the globe three times in two years, playing to almost five million people and nudging their total album sales towards fifty million. The live head count had by now been expanded to twelve, taking in an additional keyboard player, a couple of backing singers and a three-piece brass section. Guns argued with some logic that the extra manpower was needed to reproduce the subtleties and textures of the new records without having to use backing tapes.

However, some fans bemoaned the big production as being 'too cabaret' and far removed from Guns N'Roses' roots as a gut level rock 'n' roll band. More worryingly, Izzy Stradlin had begun to feel the same way, and he had also tired of Axl's unpredictability. One show in St Louis had even ended in a riot after the explosive frontman personally tackled a camera-wielding member of the audience and then aborted the concert. Fifty people were injured in the ensuing mêlée, the band's equipment was wrecked, and considerable damage was caused to the venue itself.

Guns N'Roses' show at Wembley Stadium on 31 August was to be Izzy's last – for a while at least. His

self-respect and sanity demanded that he strike out on his own, which he did rapidly, putting together his Ju Ju Hounds project and recording his own album in little over a year.

'It was very, very hard when Izzy quit,' Slash remembers. 'You never really see these things coming, and when they do happen you just have to hang in there. It becomes a survival thing. It's like losing a finger or something. You just have to keep going.'

And keep going they did. Former Jane's Addiction guitarist David Navarro reputedly turned down an offer of $2 million to replace Stradlin, and one Gilby Clarke, who'd played with LA bands Candy and Kill For Thrills and had been an acquaintance of the band since the earliest days, was to be the beneficiary of his rebuff.

After allowing Clarke just one week to familiarise himself with the set, the unending tour ground onward, crossing and re-crossing the Atlantic. Axl caused further controversy during a worldwide live TV broadcast from Paris when he tore into film star Warren Beatty who had apparently shown more than a passing interest in his current girlfriend Stephanie Seymour.

American dates that summer with Metallica were soured by a crowd riot in Montreal after Axl had ended the show after an hour, complaining of a strained voice. Earlier the same evening, Metallica had also curtailed their performance after singer James Hetfield was burned by a misfiring flamepot, and the already disgruntled audience were enraged by what they regarded as Axl's prima donna routine.

May 1992 was to provide the least likely twist of all in the always convoluted Guns N'Roses story. Despite the bucket-loads of venom thrown by both parties after the original split, Axl invited Izzy back to stand in for Gilby who had injured his hand. Even more surprisingly, Izzy accepted, and appeared at five shows. Speaking of the arrangement afterwards, though, Izzy commented that the reunion had merely reminded him why he had quit in the first place. His former band mates, meanwhile, dismayed by Izzy's financial demands for his brief return, were only too pleased to welcome back the recovered Gilby to polish off the remaining dates, and to complete work on the punk covers EP that Guns had been threatening to release almost since day one.

Of course, this being the very largest of larger-than-life outfits, the EP was ultimately expanded into a full-length album, and its intended punk rock bias was lost somewhere along the way, so that alongside band favourites by the Damned and the UK Subs, were numbers originally recorded by Nazareth, T Rex and a fifties vocal band called the Skyliners. In fact it was to be the Skyliners' song 'Since I Don't Have You' that was lifted from the album as a single cut and given the expensive video treatment. Slash is now unsure about where the original idea for a covers record came from.

'I think if you were to talk to each guy in the band individually you'd get a different story about how that one came about. It was just a bunch of songs by a bunch of bands that had been important to us in some way. We just went in and threw them down on tape without any of the pressure of having to write new material and being judged for it. That's one of the unfortunate things about being successful: every time you write a song everybody scrutinises it. *The Spaghetti Incident* [as the record was named] was just us having a good time jamming some tunes we liked. It was a tremendous release after the *...Illusion* tour.'

The release was well timed, coming at the front end of a lengthy period of relative inactivity from Guns N'Roses as a unit, which has allowed Duff to finally complete his long-toiled-over solo album *Believe In Me*; Gilby to record his excellent *Pawn Shop Guitars* opus; and Slash to record and tour with his Snakepit sideline.

'If Guns isn't working I find other places to work,' he explains. 'I guess I'm basically a workaholic. If I'm not playing somewhere, *I tend* to get into trouble.'

Though not as much trouble as the luckless Gilby, who after being a little too frank with the press about the band's internal politics, was given his cards by the fiery singer in June of 1994. Enter one Paul Huge, an old friend of Axl's who actually received a co-writing credit for 'Back Off Bitch' on *...Illusion* volume I. Although it was at first suggested that Huge would merely be a writing partner for Axl, he was brought in without the rest of the band's approval to add guitar parts to a cover of the Rolling Stones' 'Sympathy for the Devil' that Guns recorded for the Tom Cruise movie *Interview with the Vampire*. Slash especially was incensed by his partner's manoeuvre.

Following the row, speculation mounted that Axl had actually *fired* Slash and was courting Ozzy Osbourne's guitarist Zakk Wylde for a new-look Guns N'Roses. How much truth there is in this particular story remains unclear. What is certain is that Axl *was* in contact with Wylde, although it was claimed that the two were only writing together, and that there were no plans to drop anybody from Guns N'Roses. Whatever the truth is, the cold war between Slash and Axl persisted into the period when the guitarist was putting together his *It's Five O'Clock Somewhere* record with Snakepit. Axl allegedly threatened legal action against Slash, claiming that some of the songs recorded for the Snakepit album had been earmarked for Guns N'Roses' use. Slash countered by insisting that the tunes had in fact been rejected by Axl, thus clearing them for Snakepit's use.

'Guns N'Roses is pretty much always in a constant state of upheaval,' says Slash. 'There's always a situation that I'm not expecting. The way I see rock 'n' roll is that it should be simple, but for some strange reason Guns is always going through these really complex, unique situations that keep everything at a standstill. If I was to give any advice to a young musician it'd be to look out for this shit, because it comes out of nowhere, and you have to prepare yourself.'

At the time of writing Axl is busy fending off lawsuits while Duff and Matt have recorded and are gigging sporadically with an outfit called the Neurotic Outsiders – also featuring Sex Pistol Steve Jones and Duran Duran bassist John Taylor. Slash has recently announced that he has left the band, but it is believed that Axl will continue without him and record a new Guns album.

By the time you're reading this, anything could have happened. There could be a brand new Guns N'Roses album in the shops, or the most unpredictable band in the world might have dissolved for good. That's the nature of the beast. At least it's never boring.

ALBUM DISCOGRAPHY

Live?!*@ Like A Suicide (EP) (1985)

Appetite For Destruction (1987)

GN'R LIES - the Sex, the Drugs, the Violence, the Shocking Truth (1988)

Use Your Illusion Volumes I & II (1991)

The Spaghetti Incident (1993)

Believe In Me (Duff McKagan) (1993)

Pawn Shop Guitars (Gilby Clarke) (1994)

It's Five O'Clock Somewhere (Slash's Snakepit) (1995)

Neurotic Outsiders (Duff McKagan, Matt Sorum) (1996)

AEROSMITH

Aerosmith: even the mention of the name leaves a pleasant taste on the tongue.

Certainly one of the most enduring and influential bands in existence, Aerosmith can rejoice under that most auspicious of titles – legends. Throughout their long career, with its painful downs and glorious ups, a simple, unshakable faith in the healing power of rock 'n' roll has kept them in flight. Aerosmith's two protagonists, vocalist Steven Tyler and guitarist Joe Perry, have enjoyed a bittersweet relationship which has, for all its friction, inspired some of the most irresistible rock music ever made. The duo have been the equivalent of musical witch doctors, dancing with spirits and casting a spell over audiences worldwide. For Aerosmith, it's all about entertainment, and few have done it better.

Joe Perry

By the mid-nineties, Aerosmith were able to look back on over two decades of life at the top. As hedonistic as their early career was, they have managed to draw strength and sobriety from their great wealth of experience, and remain to this day one of the most sprightly and energetic live attractions around. It is from the seamless barrage of Joe Perry and Brad Whitford's guitars that this energy is born, but it manifests itself in the shape of Tyler, a man seemingly possessed both by this and by the voodoo rhythms of drummer Joey Kramer and bassist Tom Hamilton. Though Whitford, Kramer and Hamilton have always taken a back seat to the extravagant personalities of Tyler and Perry, each of them is a vital, integral cog in the great machine. Without them, the fire and the fury, the magic and the mystery just wouldn't be the same. Theirs, clearly, is a unique chemistry.

'Even now, it still gives me an incredible thrill to look over one shoulder and see Joe Perry standing there, and to look over the other and see Brad Whitford,' declares Steven Tyler. 'The chemistry and camaraderie was perfect to start with, and it's so great to be able to say that it's lasted. If anything, it's stronger now than ever.

'I can remember when I first got into music, and first got that buzz. In the fifties and sixties, I would always have the radio on, and even though you always had a really rough, crackly reception in those days, I was drawn to the sounds of the Everlys and Duane Eddy. With the Everlys, it was the harmonies that attracted me. It was so pretty and melodic. I bought five Kinks albums, and they really sealed it for me. Later on I was influenced by the Pretty Things, the Stones, the Walker Brothers and a lot of the English imports. I felt that music was in my blood.'

The five members of Aerosmith have actually been together longer than most of their audience have been on the planet. The band was formed in 1970, when Chain Reaction's Steven Tyler (born Steve Talarico on 26 March 1948 in New York) met the Jam Band's Joe Perry (born 10 September 1950 in Boston) who was working in a local ice cream parlour. Perry was interested in forming a power trio in the style of Cream, and invited Tyler to join, strangely enough as

Joey Kramer

To this day, the energy and professionalism of Aerosmith's live performances leave audiences breathless . . .

Steven Tyler

Tom Hamilton

the drummer, while Tom Hamilton played bass. The New Hampshire-based act then recruited a second guitarist, Ray Tabano, who was quickly replaced by Brad Whitford. Tyler justifiably persuaded his bandmates that they would be better off with him singing, and Joey Kramer was recruited to occupy his seat on the drum stool.

'As you go through life there are a lot of things you don't remember, but one thing that I'll never forget is my first meeting with Joe Perry,' remarks Steven. 'It's true that he was working at an ice cream parlour. It was a small-town restaurant called the Anchorage. Joe was working in the back, cooking up fries and stuff. It's hard to believe now, but he was just the same Joe Perry that we know today. He had heard that I was looking to join a band, and that was how it started. The five of us lived together in a Boston apartment, which really cemented our friendship and proved that we could work together. The other guys that lived with us had a truck which they let us borrow for gigs.'

Aerosmith's exuberant and overtly sexual live performances earned them a loyal following in the Boston area, and pretty soon their reputation translated into record company interest. Clive Davis of Columbia/CBS Records signed the band, who released their debut album *Aerosmith* in 1973. Their first single, 'Dream On', originally peaked at Number 59 in the American chart, but became a Top Ten hit when it was reissued in 1976. Living together enabled the band to work on and really perfect their live craft. In those early days, they supported such acts as the Kinks and Mott the Hoople, releasing their acclaimed second album, *Get Your Wings*, in the process.

It was their third album, *Toys In The Attic*, however, that really launched Aerosmith down the runway. Their reputation as a live act was now quite formidable. To this day, the energy and professionalism of Aerosmith's live performances leave audiences breathless, and, with hits like 'Sweet Emotion', 'Dream On' and 'Walk This Way', the band were becoming one of America's premier rock acts. The group's work rate during the seventies was quite breathtaking. They toured almost continuously for five years, pausing only to record more albums. The legendary *Rocks* provided them with their first million seller, and even the critically panned *Draw the Line* was a considerable success.

'Looking back now is strange,' reflects Steven. 'Talking about those old records is like flicking through an old photo album. You know you were there but it's often hard to remember the details. People will always say that *Rocks* and *Toys...* were our best albums of the seventies, but it's hard to say whether that's actually true. I still love all those old songs and I suppose those two albums are among our favourites. Other people might want to call them classics. For me, the best thing about them is that they remind me of where I was and what I was doing at the time.'

The only stigma that the band faced in these years was allegations that their music was too closely influenced by Led Zeppelin, or, worse, that they were nothing more than America's answer to

the Rolling Stones. Although the Stones were undoubtedly an influence, most of the accusers were more concerned with Tyler's facial resemblance to Mick Jagger, hardly a factor that he had engineered!

'In the early days, the press never had anything good to say about us,' recalls Steven. 'The comparisons to Jagger and the Stones really pissed us off at the time, but we're not concerned about it now. It's really not a bad thing to be likened to the Stones, and I've talked about it with Mick Jagger on a few occasions. I guess we both had blues influences, but mixed it up and did things our own way. "Big Ten Inch Record" and "Walk This Way" are examples of how we took a basic sound and stamped our own identity on it. Apart from that, there was the obvious fact that we looked a bit like the Stones, and there was the way that Joe and I acted on stage which some people though was a little like Mick and Keith.'

In 1978 and '79, Aerosmith gave a series of legendary performances at various music festivals, showcasing their superhuman capabilities as a live act. Vast numbers of fans and potential fans witnessed the gigs, including 250,000 at the California Jam 2 Festival. The Texas Jam followed, along with the 1979 California Music Festival. At the same time, the band were appearing as the bad guys in a film adaptation of *Sergeant Pepper's Lonely Hearts Club Band*, to which they also contributed a cover of the Lennon/McCartney song 'Come Together'. To this day, many of the band's younger fans believe that this is an Aerosmith original, so popular has it proved.

Unfortunately, the more Aerosmith stayed out on the road, the more they turned to drugs and alcohol for relief. As their success sky rocketed, so their dependency and notoriety deepened. At the time, these hedonistic trappings were seen as synonymous with the glamour of life in the fast lane. In retrospect, Aerosmith are lucky to have survived.

Tyler and Perry were humorously dubbed 'the Toxic Twins' in recognition of their knife-edge lifestyle.

'Our live act obviously suffered as a consequence,' reveals Steven, 'but it's important to remember that things were different then. It was normal to behave like that. Kids would have to watch me stumbling around on stage, falling over, not being able to hit the notes, but all that was a symptom of the times. I'm lucky that I managed to live through it.'

Stresses in the band worsened, and simple differences in personality suddenly looked like insurmountable problems.

As the band released the uneasy *Night in the Ruts*, Perry decided that he could no longer work with Tyler, and left to form the Joe Perry Project. Two months later, Brad Whitford jumped ship as well.

'The split was all to do with our drugs mentality,' admits the frontman. 'The friendship that we had was overtaken by our need to do drugs. Joe wouldn't share his dope with me which meant a hell of a lot at the time. Things were thrown about and I just said, "Fuck you, I'll do this band without you." I couldn't even imagine life without a band around me.'

Aerosmith limped on half-heartedly. Guitarists Jimmy Crespo and Rick Dufay had replaced the departed duo, but it was plain for fans and critics alike to see that Aerosmith's heart and soul had been ripped out. Problems were exacerbated by Tyler's rapidly declining health, and it was no surprise to anyone that 1980's *Rock in a Hard Place* failed to capture the swagger of old. The band's wings had been well and truly broken. For four years they struggled with personal problems and waning record sales, before Perry and Whitford returned to the fold, and a new record deal, with Geffen, was struck. During his sabbatical from the group, Perry had

Joe Perry

Tyler and Perry let the music do the talking

Tom Hamilton

released two albums, while Whitford had joined an ill-fated venture with former Ted Nugent Band member Derek St Holmes. Both were relieved to have their day jobs back again.

'It was a great relief for all of us,' says Tyler. 'To see Joe Perry and Brad Whitford back where they truly belonged was a great thrill. Right now, I can still feel that thrill, knowing what they turned into and the way that they can perform. Although I loved Jimmy Crespo and Rick Dufay, it simply wasn't the same. The old camaraderie was missing.'

These hopeful signs were tempered by the faltering health of both Tyler and Perry. After the release of their reunion album, *Done With Mirrors*, the pair embarked on a successful rehabilitation programme. The idea of a 'clean' Tyler and Perry confounded many who had become used to hearing reports of the vocalist collapsing on stage, but clean they were, and clean they remained.

'Stopping a heroin habit is not easy,' shudders Steven. 'When we did *Done With Mirrors*, we were still addicted, even though we pretended we weren't. We kept sneaking fixes. But having to rush off to someone's house to get drugs in the middle of the night is not a good way to live your life. Running out of blow at three in the morning, and getting a cab into town, *needing* more, sleeping in Washington Square – that's when the time comes to put the brakes on. At the worst of it, I had virtually become a street kid. We did thirty to forty days in rehab, and we had to go back a few times after that. We had to learn to do without.

'I tried to think about the energy I would have if I wasn't coughing every day. I thought about how much better the music would be if I could transfer my energy to that. I thought about getting through airport customs without having to worry about the drugs I had stashed in my case. It was really traumatic. This had been a way of life for me for the last twenty years, but now it had to stop.'

Neither of the so-called Toxic Twins has touched their particular toxin since. Other figures in the public eye have successfully overcome drug and alcohol problems, but few have returned from the abyss as convincingly as Tyler and Perry. With their talents set free to soar, the rest of the Aerosmith story is simply a list of triumphs, each apparently greater than the last. Like Jagger and Richards, or Page and Plant, the two key figures of Aerosmith enjoy an occasionally strained but musically mesmeric relationship. It has manifested itself in some of the most boisterous and influential rock albums ever made.

Aerosmith returned to the public consciousness with the help of rappers Run DMC, and their radically re-worked version of 'Walk This Way'. Whilst the video secured heavy MTV rotation, 1987's most popular new band, Guns N'Roses, were citing Aerosmith as a pivotal influence in almost every interview. The public's appetite for destruction was whetted for a new album from the Boston-based veterans.

Kiss this Aerosmith live

Permanent Vacation proved to be just the tonic that the band's supporters had been craving. It was a timely reminder of the old Aerosmith colour and spice, each track incorporating a different flavour, but all united by Tyler and Perry's renewed chemistry. Sassy, saucy rockers like 'Dude (Looks Like a Lady)' and 'Rag Doll' were complemented by the rich, orchestra-backed balladry of 'Angel', while 'I'm Down' was another storming interpretation of a Beatles classic. Above all, the album had a celebratory feel to it. This was the work of a band back from the brink, and sounding better then ever.

'Considering our drugs mentality, *Done With Mirrors* was never really finished,' confesses Steven. 'The music on that record really suffered. *Permanent Vacation*, however, was a different matter altogether. We were not only clean, but we had rediscovered what it was that had made this band special in the first place. It was a lot of things, really. *Permanent Vacation* proved something to us, and made us realise that the old spirit was back. It turned out to be just the tip of the iceberg.'

The album returned Aerosmith to greatness in America, where they were attracting a new, younger generation of fans who had been inspired by the likes of Bon Jovi and Guns N'Roses to investigate the forefathers of the movement. Europe, however, would take a little longer to respond. Tyler and Perry paved the way for their next album, 1989's *Pump*, by joining Bon Jovi on stage at Milton Keynes Bowl to sing 'Walk This Way'.

'I loved the way that the whole Los Angeles scene and a lot of the really popular rock bands of the late eighties started citing us as an influence,' recalls Steven. 'It was very flattering that people wanted to copy our sound and our image. There was a renewal of interest in the band which was amazing because we weren't even sure if people would still like us.'

Steven Tyler

We were coming up with material that was a consolidation between the old and the new. As a band, we had always been kinda "underground", and we'd never really been a hit singles kinda band, until now. Until Guns N'Roses did their version of "Mama Kin", no one had ever covered an Aerosmith song. It was cool.'

With both European and American audiences warming to their cause, *Pump* stormed the charts all over the world, spawning several hit singles in the process. 'Love In An Elevator' was a huge international hit, and was accompanied by a typically suggestive video. In contrast, 'Janie's Got a Gun', another major hit, contained messages about child abuse. Overall, *Pump* proved that Aerosmith had revitalised their career, and that this time they were here to stay. Though they were now in their forties, they were continuing to improve their songwriting, and had honed their live act into one of the finest on the circuit.

Pump had a harder edge than *Permanent Vacation*, highlighting the scorching guitar work of Messrs Perry and Whitford. Thunderous tracks like 'Young Lust' and 'F.I.N.E.' proved that Aerosmith could still rock with the best of them, whilst the ballad 'What It Takes', another U.S. Top Ten hit, showed their more emotional side, and wrought a heart-breaking delivery from Tyler.

'You could say that the songs on *Pump* were written in an unusual way,' reflects Steven. 'With some of the songs, we just started jamming to see what came out. That's how we like to write, but I guess it's not how most bands would approach it. When in the studio I'll sometimes start playing drums again, because that's often where things can start. "Boogie Man", for example, which was recorded during the *Pump* sessions and eventually got released on the *Get a Grip* album, was actually recorded as it was being written. We never sat down and thought it through. It just rolled out!'

Magic and spontaneity in the studio quickly transformed into immense audience demand, and

Joe Perry

Aerosmith embarked on a lengthy world tour in support of *Pump*. In August 1990, they made their debut at the Donington Monsters of Rock Festival as special guests of Whitesnake, where they were joined on stage by Jimmy Page. By common consent, they stole much of the headliners' thunder that day, and in 1994 they were back to headline the event themselves. At the end of their 163-date tour, they had sold 7 million copies of *Pump*, bringing their career total to a resounding 28 million. For their efforts they won numerous awards and honours, including a Grammy for 'Janie's Got a Gun' and an SKC Music Award for Most Outstanding Band.

At the end of their 163-date tour, they had sold 7 million copies of *Pump*, bringing their career total to a resounding 28 million.

Aerosmith delighted at the prospect of playing Donington. Honestly...

Tom Hamilton

Tyler and Perry

Steven: 'It's hard to say whether the *Pump* tour was the most satisfying experience of the band's career. It's hard to compare. We weren't actually aware of how successful our record was at the time. That only came to light afterwards. The audiences, though, were amazing. I just love the energy that comes off the crowd, and that really helps me through. The *Pump* tour also gave us the chance to play in various South American countries we'd never even been to before.

'We enjoyed a whole load of new experiences. Like playing at Donington for the first time, and having Jimmy Page come out on stage with us. We also played an amazing gig at the Marquee club in London, and Jimmy jammed with us there too. What an amazing experience – I can still remember seeing Led Zeppelin at the Tea Party in Boston way back in 1970.'

Despite their advancing years, the group have continued moving forward at a rapid pace. 1993's *Get a Grip* was again produced by Bruce Fairbairn, who had worked on both *Permanent Vacation* and *Pump*. Though it failed to capture the intensity of the latter or the diversity of the former, it still harvested some great songs, proving once again (as if any proof were needed) that Tyler and Perry had not lost their touch.

'After *Get a Grip*, we had the opportunity to headline Donington,' remembers Steven. 'This band has always thrived on the big occasion. We have a long history of playing big festival-type shows in front of massive crowds. It's still a complete thrill to play a show like that. A lot of people assume that I don't get nervous any more, but I *always* do. If it's the first show of a long tour, or a big show like Donington, it's only natural to be a little scared. By the time you get to the hundredth show, things are a little better, but it's still nerve-wracking. To be honest, I feel more nervous doing big shows now than I did in the seventies. The audience is so vast and seems to stretch so far away that you feel you're being examined under a microscope. You become really self-conscious. In a way I preferred the kind of shows we did in the seventies when the audience seemed to be all around you. You felt you were nestling in the womb of it all.'

STEVEN TYLER

Favourite album: That's the hardest question of all time to answer, but I'll say *Smile* by the Beach Boys.

First gig attended: Chubby Checker at Atlantic City in 1958. Let's twist again, baby!

Most embarrassing tour story: Ha! Loads of things have happened. I would say that walking straight off the stage into the musicians' pit is hard to beat. This was before the days of mosh pits, and there was a long way to fall.

Favourite food: Anything involving peanut butter is usually good. Also, raspberry jelly and ice cream.

Causes supported: I will support anything that saves lives.

What would surprise someone most about you? I used to be a drummer, and still play from time to time.

If your house was burning, what would you save first? My coffee espresso machine!

As the group undertook their most successful world tour to date, they enjoyed international hits with 'Livin' on the Edge', 'Cryin' and 'Crazy'. The video for 'Crazy' became an MTV favourite, and featured Tyler's daughter Liv, herself a successful model and actress, as the storyline's protagonist.

After a break, Aerosmith returned once again to the studio. 'We're a pubic hair's length away from getting everything done,' chuckles Steven, when asked about the new album, *Nine Lives*, released in March 1997. 'I'm really happy about how it's turned out. It's different enough to the last one to make me scared, and it's new enough to make me worry about whether everyone's gonna dig it. We have at least three new songs that are really unusual, completely unlike anything on the last album. One of the things that I love most about being in this band is that we're never afraid to take risks. We get together on something and try to approach it in different ways. Weird stuff comes out. But people that love the band shouldn't worry – it's still gonna be a cool Aerosmith record. It's just something new.'

Interest in the band has inevitably centred on Steven Tyler and Joe Perry. This has partly been due to their Jagger/Richards-style relationship, and partly due to the notoriety of their past excesses. Ironically, this has worked in their favour, and may be one of the secrets of their longevity. Tyler, in particular, was born to front a rock 'n' roll band, and has happily shouldered his share of the publicity. Whitford, Hamilton and Kramer have been able to stay away from the limelight, focusing instead on their musicianship. Although record reviews have occasionally given Joe Perry the credit for guitar parts played by Brad Whitford, the situation has generally been to the band's mutual benefit.

Joe rips it up live

'On the whole,' says Steven, 'it does seem to have been Joe and myself that the media have chosen to highlight. That isn't because we kinda pushed the other guys to the back, which is what some people think. It was just the way that it happened. Everyone seemed to pick up on the look that I had, and the style that Joe brought to the guitar, and that somehow became the band's image, the thing that everyone came back to.

'In the seventies it did become a problem. Joe and myself were appearing on the cover of *Rolling Stone* magazine, and the others weren't. It happened a few times. Now it's not so bad. They understand it a lot better. I'd much

prefer Aerosmith to be perceived as a group thing, but I understand the power of images. It's always gonna be a problem, but everyone handles it well. We certainly don't fight about it.'

Aerosmith are a highly respected act who have rarely been out of favour with either fans or critics. Though drug abuse and personality clashes almost destroyed them in the early eighties, their tenacity and resilience has rendered them once again amongst the world's favourite bands. Few bands have enjoyed such an enduring appeal, and indeed, it is hard to think of any at all who can still boast their original line-up after twenty-seven years of recording and touring.

Such experience has welded Aerosmith into an incredible unit. Their live shows, always their forte, have been as spellbinding and vivacious in the nineties as they ever were in their supposed seventies heyday. It has certainly not been an easy ride for any of them. The late Mark Putterford titled his biography of the band *The Fall and Rise of Aerosmith*, and rarely has a book been more appropriately christened. Having triumphed over immense adversity, Aerosmith have truly earned their wings.

ALBUM DISCOGRAPHY:

Aerosmith (1973)
Get Your Wings (1974)
Toys in the Attic (1975)
Rocks (1976)
Draw the Line (1977)
Live! Bootleg (1978)
Night in the Ruts (1979)
Greatest Hits (1980)
Rock in a Hard Place (1982)
Done With Mirrors (1985)
Classics Live (1986)
Permanent Vacation (1987)
Anthology (1988)
Pump (1989)
Get a Grip (1993)
Big Ones (Greatest Hits) (1994)
Nine Lives (1997)

OZZY OSBOURNE

The crackle of static, the buzz of electricity. From somewhere deep in the shadows beyond the ilken whirls of smoke, a funereal tide of classical nusic begins to peal out. A dark, slightly hunched igure appears silhouetted in the middle of the stage. His arms are held out at both sides, and a spotlight weeps over his twisted grimace. Suddenly, the air erupts as if rent apart by thunderbolts. The audience ecoils as a supernova of light and noise rushes hrough the hot air. 'Let's go crazy!' shrieks the figure. t could be 1968. It could be now. Were serpents to ain down from the sky, the audience would still not hift their eyes from this strange demigod.

He is Ozzy Osbourne, and this is one of the most nemorable and oft-repeated scenes in rock history. Not much can compare to the atmosphere of an Ozzy jig. This is because Ozzy is the greatest living egend in metal. When he and three other partners n crime emerged from the junk-strewn streets of downtown Birmingham, few could have oreseen the sheer enormity of what would be created. Now, almost thirty years after he first psychotic ravings of this heavy netal thunder bringer, his crazy train is still clattering down the tracks.

'It's a passion,' Ozzy told Vanessa Warwick from *Headbangers' Ball.* There's no sex or drugs or anything quite like rock 'n' roll. I would pay o get that buzz. I want to feel the way that I try to make my audience feel.'

For Ozzy himself, it has been a long, difficult ride that he is fortunate to have survived. In his wake, however, lies what some people call 'heavy metal' and others just call 'rock'; a vast and diverse culture upon which many have based their lives. More than anything, this is why Ozzy Osbourne is looked up to with such awe and devotion. It is tempting to believe that without Ozzy there would be none of this at all.

'I don't see my music as being any better then anyone else's,' is Ozzy's modest contention. 'I can only describe it as a labour of love. I don't look on myself as being this great, important figure, and I try not to treat anyone any differently to how I'd wish to be treated myself. The performer in me is on a mission to get every last one of those people in the audience jumping about. That's what it's all about – having a good time and giving the kids a good time.'

His arms are held out at both sides and a spotlight sweeps over his twisted grimace. Suddenly the air erupts as if rent apart by thunderbolts.

The audience recoils as a supernova of light and noise rushes through the hot air.

Let's go crazy shrieks the figure.

Little of this grand scheme was planned by the man himself. He stumbled upon it unwittingly, and dealt with it the best he could. Born on 3 December 1948, the teenage Osbourne drifted from job to job, and in a state of disillusionment turned his hand to petty theft. In 1967, he formed Black Sabbath with three other disgruntled local youths. From dismal beginnings, the group rapidly became internationally successful, and are regarded as the single greatest influence in the history of metal. **Ozzy, with his tearful wail and hysterical, headbanging, wild-eyed stage manner, was the physical manifestation of the new genre.**

'I was desperate to find a way out, and being in a band seemed a good way of doing that,' recalls Ozzy, speaking from his Buckinghamshire home. 'When the Beatles happened, it set something off inside me and I just got sucked into the lifestyle. I look back now and think how incredible it's all been. I'm forty-eight now and I live in the most beautiful house, not at all in keeping with my background.

'I had little education. In fact, school was the worst thing that ever happened to me, because I suffer from dyslexia. At the time I was at school, they didn't have a word called "dyslexic", you were just called "thick" instead. I don't mean to blow my own trumpet, but I've since found out that many dyslexic people are very talented in other areas.'

By January 1979, when Ozzy finally parted company with Sabbath, the band had released eight albums plus one compilation. Amongst these were the likes of *Paranoid*, *Sabbath Bloody Sabbath* and *Vol IV*, seminal albums that achieved international acclaim and launched the careers of countless other metal bands. **The music was heavy as lead, full of mysticism and macabre lyrical angles.** Many justifiably give credit to Tony Iommi for patenting that grinding guitar sound, but none of it would have been possible without Ozzy, a presence so enormous and a voice so unique that Sabbath were never able to recapture their early glory without him. Ozzy remembers the dramatic ascent of Sabbath in vivid detail.

'We were initially managed by a guy in Birmingham called Jim Simpson. I remember jumping in a Transit van to go and do our regular stint at the Star Club in Hamburg which was great for me, because that's where the Beatles used to play. On the way to the ferry we stopped off and made the first Black Sabbath album. We just played our songs in some basement and recorded them. Then, after eight weeks in Hamburg, we came home and Jim said, "Come over and see me – I've got your album cover and it's on the Vertigo label!" When I saw that spooky-looking chick on the cover, I was totally stunned.

'Next thing I knew, I was at a club called the Elbow Room in Birmingham, and Jim tells me that we've just gone into the British chart at Number 17. **My first record royalty payment was for £105 and I thought I'd won the lottery. I'd never even seen that much money before.** After that, it just exploded and I've never looked back. Every record I've sung on, with the exception of the last album I did with Sabbath, has gone platinum. As you become more successful, you change without realising it. For example, I've ended up with that many bloody suits that if they were to stop making suits tomorrow I'd still have enough to see me through to the end of the next century.'

For Osbourne, the Sabbath years passed in a blur of drug-taking and alcoholism. Like so many stars in the seventies, Ozzy had wholeheartedly embraced a lifestyle that was both hedonistic and self-destructive in the extreme. His problems, particularly with alcohol, were to continue throughout the eighties, and the toll on his health was considerable. These problems go some way to explaining his often controversial public behaviour. Most notorious of all was an incident in 1981, when Ozzy bit the head off a live dove in front of an assembly of record company executives. The press, thoroughly fascinated by Osbourne's 'madman' persona, have never allowed this incident to fade into history.

'You know what? I never read a fucking thing any more,' Ozzy reveals. 'It's not because I'm dyslexic, it's because it spoils my day. Some journalists spend their time fishing around for sensationalist stories, trying to make names for themselves. In America I was at one stage getting more press than the President. Even recently, I read an article in which I'm supposed to have said that I hated

The much missed Randy Rhoads

[former guitarist] Zakk Wylde. I don't hate anyone and I certainly never said that about Zakk, who I like immensely.'

A cynical press could do nothing to halt Ozzy's considerable musical output. His first post-Sabbath album was the legendary *Blizzard of Ozz*, which featured several timeless Ozzy classics, including 'Crazy Train', 'Mr Crowley', 'I Don't Know' and 'Suicide Solution'. In California, Ozzy had discovered a brilliant young guitarist named Randy Rhoads. In his short career, Rhoads was hailed as one of the most prodigious talents to have ever lived. His playing was not only technically flawless, but had a brutally incendiary edge that imbued Ozzy's songs with their customary thunder. Rhoads was a quiet, humble guy, a total contrast to Tony Iommi's domineering personality.

'I actually lived with Randy for about eighteen months in an apartment in London,' says Ozzy. 'While I was busy getting drunk, he used to travel all over the country sightseeing. He'd come back with loads of miniature model trains which he absolutely loved.

'Every town we'd visit, he'd pick up the telephone directory, find a classical guitar tutor and go for a lesson. He was an incredibly dedicated musician.

Ozzy rejoices in his madman persona

Those early tours of Britain with Randy were so much fun, staying in bed-and-breakfast accommodation, getting drunk, breaking into the kitchens at four in the morning and having fry-ups, that kinda thing.'

Ozzy and Randy became great friends as well as partners in mayhem. By the time they released a second album, *Diary of a Madman*, they had upgraded their ambitions, and displayed the artistic cohesion to match. Tragically, Randy's explosive talent was snuffed out forever when he was killed in a private plane crash in 1982. A devastated Ozzy, then in the middle of a U.S. tour, struggled on, using a succession of temporary guitarists. With Brad Gillis, a double live album of old Sabbath standards was released, titled *Talk of the Devil*. But no one could replace Randy. Indeed, Ozzy has never enjoyed a similarly stable working relationship with a guitarist since that fateful day in 1982.

'I've still got happy memories of touring those first two solo albums,' he affirms. 'We were just like a bunch of big kids let out of our cage and allowed to go mad. Then, of course, Randy was tragically killed. I remember saying to Bob Daisley, our bassist at the time, that there are some people in my life who I just sense have something bad in store for them, and Randy was among them. He was just too good a guy to last. The irony is that I was always the one getting legless, jumping off cliffs and taking risks, and yet he was the one that died. He was an amazing talent. A lot of guitarists use their instrument as a piece of stagecraft, whereas Randy treated the guitar as an extension of his personality and his emotions.'

Bark at the Moon, released in 1983, saw Ozzy adopt a werewolf-inspired horror movie image, an idea that tied in nicely with his already larger than life reputation. By this time, he had married his personal manager, Sharon Arden, who freed him from his old record deal and signed him with CBS in America and Epic in Britain. Sharon's expertise and influence have proved to be indispensable. Not only has she masterminded his career, but has gradually

'The most I can remember about Live Aid is how grossly overweight I was,' quips Ozzy.

curbed his many excesses, probably saving his life in the process. As if that were not enough, she is also the mother of his three children.

Ozzy happily pays tribute to the woman who has changed his life: 'Sharon comes from a very different background to mine, and has taught me a great deal. As a manager, she puts me in my place. It's not like a Paul and Linda [McCartney] relationship, with loads of veggie pies involved. Without my wife I wouldn't be talking to you now – I'd either be dead or on some park bench somewhere. Sharon is not the kind of woman who just peels potatoes and changes nappies. In fact, when people talk about my influence, they should also talk about Sharon's influence. Aside from my career, she's also been a very positive influence for women in general on a managerial level.

'For instance, when we went to Japan we discovered that women there are basically used for sex and cooking. They walk three feet behind their men and are almost like slaves. So I go out there with a woman manager and their eyeballs nearly popped out. Nowadays, women are accepted more in all kinds of industries and pretty soon we're gonna be wondering where all the guys went.'

Following *Bark at the Moon* and an extensive tour, Ozzy endured a stay in the Betty Ford rehabilitation clinic. He returned in 1985, reforming Black Sabbath for a one-off date at the Live Aid extravaganza. Rather than acting as a catalyst for a more lengthy reunion, the experience seemed to drive the original members further apart. Much acrimony still remained between Osbourne and Iommi. He did, however, renew his friendship with bassist Geezer Butler, who was later to join Ozzy's band.

'The most I can remember about Live Aid is how grossly overweight I was,' quips Ozzy.

Ozzy's own career was continuing to pay huge dividends. His 1986 album, *The Ultimate Sin*, was a Top Ten success on both sides of the Atlantic, and prompted the band to undertake their biggest and most ambitious live shows to date. Ozzy had

Ozzy centre with Metallica

Ozzy with guitarist
Jake E Lee

surrounded himself with glamorous but superbly talented musicians, and rounded off the year with a thrilling headline appearance at the Donington Monsters of Rock Festival.

'The time that we did *Bark at the Moon* and *The Ultimate Sin* is really foggy,' he confesses. 'After Randy's death, I just went on a serious drugs and alcohol bender. It's terrible to admit it, but I really can't remember much about the period when Jake E Lee was in the band, because I was out of my fucking head all the time. It was all day, every day. In that respect, success did not equal happiness.'

With the controversial figure of Ozzy Osbourne now standing proud as the king of metal, media vultures began to circle overhead. Ozzy's popularity may well have made him a household name, but his addictive personality and sometimes outrageous antics made him a vulnerable target for critics. Ozzy was suddenly vilified as a public anti-hero, a demonic entity liable to bite the heads off babies.

Ozzy was looked on as the personification of all that was 'evil' in heavy metal. It was even suggested that he was a servant of Satan. In reality, the only demon that Ozzy was on familiar terms with was that of alcoholism. His behaviour under the influence of drink only added fuel to the fire.

'I got into a terrible state,' rues Ozzy. 'Please remember, I actually *saw* the fucking crash that killed Randy. No matter what I did, I just couldn't get it out of my mind. So I started drinking around the clock instead. I can't really explain it even now – I just can't find the words. You see these things on the news all the time, plane crashes and terrorist bombings, and although you think it's awful, you still can't really imagine it happening. When Randy was killed, I could actually smell the burning gasoline and I witnessed the entire horrific thing in its entirety.

'I always had an alcohol problem. As a young kid who suddenly had bags of money, I just thought, "Great, now I can buy as much booze as I want." I never even considered that it might become a problem. I just accepted it as a way of living. There must be a guardian angel watching over me because I've cheated death so many times. I'll probably have the most stupid death of all when I do go. I'll probably get hit by a low-flying pigeon or something.'

Adding to Ozzy's woes has been the fact that various parents have taken him to court, claiming that his music has incited their children to commit suicide. This theory, bizarre in the extreme, established nothing other than the absurd levels of anti-Ozzy hysteria. Thankfully, Osbourne's name has been cleared on every occasion. Rather then flying into a rage over such treatment, which would only have made things worse, Ozzy has always looked to the comical side, responding with his traditionally dry, self-deprecating sense of humour. When an investigative television programme filmed a documentary on the 'links' between music and satanism, Ozzy willingly gave an interview. He was asked, in deadly serious tones, whether he had ever attempted to conjure up the devil. In reliably amusing style, the long-suffering star assured us that he had enough problems conjuring himself out of bed in the morning.

Ozzy during the photo sessions for the Talk of the Devils album

'I wouldn't say that Zakk picked up where Randy left off, but he was certainly a fantastic player,' says Ozzy. 'He could play any style brilliantly; heavier than Tony Iommi one minute and Country & Western the next. The only trouble was that I was never really sure which style was really in his heart. After *No More Tears*, I was amazed when he did a huge U-turn and made that *Pride and Glory* album [Zakk's one-off side project]. It was the equivalent of me releasing an album of Christmas carols: "Oh Come All Ye Faithful" by Ozzy Osbourne!

'It was also good to work with Geezer again. Even when a relationship breaks up you try to remember the good things about it and forget the other half, all the disappointments and arguments.'

Touring to promote *No Rest for the Wicked* saw Ozzy, Zakk, Geezer and drummer Randy Castillo gel into a formidable unit. The new songs were quintessential Ozzy, and Zakk would tear into the old Sabbath material like an old hand. For Ozzy himself, however, the longer the tour continued, the worse became the decline in his health and state of mind. The irresistible lure of the demon alcohol again held him helpless in its grip. In a most regrettable incident, a drunken Ozzy threatened his wife. When he became aware of his actions he felt shamed and defeated, and immediately checked himself into detox.

Ozzy's follow-up to *The Ultimate Sin* was the aptly titled *No Rest for the Wicked*, released in 1989. On this album he was reunited with bassist Butler, and in Zakk Wylde had recruited another extraordinary young guitarist. In terms of performance, Wylde was beyond criticism. His explosive style dominated the album, and marked him out as a major star of the future. Although Wylde is no longer part of Ozzy's band, he remained a part of the line-up for longer than any other guitarist, even playing on the 1995 album, *Ozzmosis*. Despite an age difference of nearly twenty years, Zakk has provided Ozzy with his most stable working relationship since the halcyon days of Rhoads. In 1987, Ozzy honoured the late guitarist with the release of *Tribute*, a magnificent live album recorded on the *Diary of a Madman* tour.

Despite his own considerable charity work, Ozzy was himself a victim of the vices that he had warned others so vehemently against. DJ Tommy Vance, aware that the star had become depressed and unstable, played the Sabbath classic 'Hard Road' and appealed for fans to send Ozzy messages of support. An onslaught of encouraging fan mail ensued, and with Sharon's continued support, Ozzy's determination to beat his addiction trebled.

'You can have the World Cup on your shelf, a billion platinum discs on your wall and all the riches in the world, but when you hit a brick wall it still hurts just as much,' states Ozzy. 'In life, I've had a pretty damn good run, and I've been helped

Madman turned family man

enormously by all my friends and the fans who have supported me. I live for those people and I consider myself very fortunate. I hope I haven't made any enemies and if I have, I'm sorry. Although I worry about things going wrong, I still live for that moment when I go out on stage. I never go up there and take the piss out of people that have paid to see me.'

After a relatively quiet year, Ozzy returned in 1991 with the spectacular *No More Tears*. It was the best solo album he had ever recorded, and returned him in style to the world stage. 'Hellraiser' and the autobiographical 'Desire' were spellbinding, charging rockers, Ozzy's heartfelt wail and Zakk's musclebound guitar sharpened and rounded by a perfect production. The album also threw up some superb introspective moments like 'Road to Nowhere' and 'Mama, I'm Coming Home', as well as zany horror-movie metalfests like 'Zombie Stomp' and 'Mr Tinkertrain'. The first single to be lifted from the album was the title track, an epic, rolling tune with an insistent, throbbing heartbeat. The video, featuring a woman swimming in a room full of her own tears, proved popular on MTV. Ozzy had thrown off the shackles of his former notoriety.

'Recording *No More Tears* was certainly one of the happiest times. We all sat down as a team and agreed on the type of album we wanted to make. It was one of the few times in my career when we were all focused on the one goal. I don't play an instrument, and instead I have a brain that tortures me with new tunes and melodies. With *No More Tears* we tended to work the songs out on piano before transferring them to guitar, and on "A.V.H", you'll notice some of Zakk's Southern Rock influences coming through. Zakk was always clowning around, never serious for a second, but he always had the patience to sit down and work on ideas.'

Throughout the nineties, Ozzy has toured sporadically, allowing himself sufficient time off. In the past, most of his problems have been precipitated by being out on the road too long. Now, instead of hurtling recklessly from one tour to the next, he is taking things at a more comfortable pace. After all, Ozzy Osbourne is not in a position where he has anything left to prove. It was this reason, and also the fear of committing himself to too strenuous a task, that prevented Ozzy from undertaking a reunion Black Sabbath tour. After much consideration, Ozzy backed out at the last minute.

Much has been made of Ozzy's so-called 'retirement'. The reality is that Ozzy has only retired from the rigorously enforced schedule of the music industry's treadmill. His career is no longer dictated by external forces. While the money-making wheels of industry endlessly grind, Ozzy takes a back seat, recording new songs or going out on tour when he feels like it. He is in it, basically, for fun. After a long

Ozzy in no mood for retirement

ALBUM DISCOGRAPHY:

WITH BLACK SABBATH:

Black Sabbath (1970)

Paranoid 1971)

Master of Reality (1971)

Black Sabbath Volume IV (1972)

Sabbath Bloody Sabbath (1974)

Sabotage (1975)

Technical Ecstasy (1976)

Never Say Die (1978)

SOLO:

Blizzard of Ozz (1980)

Diary of a Madman (1981)

Talk of the Devil (1982)

Bark at the Moon (1983)

The Ultimate Sin (1986)

Tribute (1987)

No Rest for the Wicked (1989)

Just Say Ozzy (1990)

No More Tears (1991)

Live and Loud (1994)

Ozzmosis (1995)

spell away from touring, largely due to indecision over the Sabbath situation, Ozzy returned in 1995 with a new album, *Ozzmosis*. Paradoxically, when it was time to tour, Ozzy renounced the usual policy of playing at least five songs from the new album, instead delighting his fans with a 'greatest hits' set, and completely ignoring *Ozzmosis*. Starting at the beginning with 'Paranoid', the gigs were a fond look back at Ozzy's rollercoaster career. Reports that Ozzy has discovered God, however, are slightly inaccurate...

'I was conned into that,' he explains. 'These people came into my house to interview me for a documentary, and they edited it so that the way it came out made me look like some kind of born again Christian. I've never had anything to do with satanism or any of that rubbish, but at the same time I am not a born again Christian. I'm just Ozzy. The audience is my spiritual experience.

'I still live it and I still love it. Now that I'm no longer on the booze, I've become something of a recluse. I don't ever seem to go out, so I need the excitement of touring and playing to audiences to sustain me. In the old days I'd be embarrassed about what I might have said or done the night before, but now I just try to take one day at a time. That's how I survive.'

The line-up of Ozzy's band at the time of writing, which features guitarist Joe Holmes, bassist Robert Trujillo and drummer Mike Bordin, the latter on loan from Faith No More, have achieved an enviable sense of brotherhood. The day after co-headlining Donington in 1996, Ozzy enthused about his new band to Vanessa for *Headbangers' Ball*: 'With my current band, we have a motto: "When you leave the stage, you leave the gig behind,"' he revealed. 'We don't want anyone accusing someone of playing the wrong note or something, because it's over and you can't re-do it. The band I have now is one of the nicest bunch of guys I've ever known...I'm really happy with it.'

As he edges towards his fifties, Ozzy Osbourne's future is exactly what he would make it. If he decides to tour again he is safe in the knowledge that there will be countless numbers of fans of all ages ready to support him. If he decides the time has come to bow out, then he has the equilibrium of his family life to cushion the fall. Decades of bodily abuse have not left Ozzy unscathed. His hands tremble slightly and there is a barely detectable slur to his speech. Nevertheless, the act of overcoming such a deep-seated and longstanding addiction is the act of a brave man and a deserving hero. Ozzy Osbourne is all of that and so much more.

Indeed, as we approach the millennium Ozzy is breaking new ground with his Ozz Fests across America, featuring an awesome line-up of cutting edge metal bands supporting his own legendary headlining show. Ozzy is also launching his own record label, Ozz Records, to help up-and-coming rock bands. The legend lives on...

OZZY OSBOURNE

Favourite album: *Sergeant Pepper's Lonely Hearts Club Band* by the Beatles.

Most embarrassing tour story: My voice going completely dead on me at a gig in Vancouver in 1996. It was the first and only time I've ever walked off stage.

Favourite food: I'm a creature of habit, but I also go through lots of fads. My latest fad is toasted crumpets and beans. Then I tend to go on to brown rice, and then red meat. To be honest, I don't eat for enjoyment. I just eat to get the job done.

Hobbies: My idea of a relaxing night in is sitting in front of the old box with a glass of Pepsi and a fine cigar.

Causes supported: Anything that promotes the education of AIDS Awareness.

If your house was burning, what would you save first? Well, apart from my wife and kids, it would have to be my dogs.

METALLICA

'I always pictured us as being a small, underground band,' shrugs Kirk Hammett, guitarist in one of the biggest bands in the world. 'I thought we'd just play clubs, theatres and stuff like that. The biggest bands at the time were Van Halen, Def Leppard and Mötley Crüe. We were so much more aggressive and extreme.'

Fourteen years and millions of album sales later, Hammett is now approached by kids in oversized Metallica T-shirts who ask why they don't make albums like 1983's viciously pounding *Kill 'Em All* any more.

'I feel like telling them, "Do you realise that you were two years old when that album came out?" ' he laughs. 'It's unbelievable, really, because I always thought an album like that would be too much for a mass audience to lock on to.'

Wrong. And with Metallica having mutated over the years, becoming more commercially acceptable while retaining that essential heavier-than-thou darkness, the stadiums of the world can barely hold them.

The story begins back in Los Angeles, May 1981, with the meeting of teenagers Lars Ulrich and James Hetfield, through a local newspaper ad placed by the former. Lars was the son of a Danish professional tennis player; he had already travelled the world and was rarely short of cash. James was more of an enigma, and it wasn't until a decade later that his frustrated childhood emerged via songs like 'The God That Failed'.

James Hetfield

The duo shared a need for sonic speed, a love of the New Wave of British Heavy Metal (NWOBHM for short), and the urge to forge something ugly from their adolescence. So they started a garage band and called it Metallica.

Enter a lead guitarist with an attitude as fiery as his hair, Dave Mustaine, along with guitarist Floyd Grant, whose tenure in the band was short. This line-up recorded a vicious little tune called 'Hit the Lights' for a compilation called *Metal Massacre*.

James played bass on that one, although as the album proceeded to make a fair dent in the underground metal sector, bassist Ron McGovney assumed that duty. Ron was doomed, however, because Metallica had their eye on a fine, flare-wearing bassist named Cliff Burton, strutting his stuff in a San Francisco band, Trauma. They wanted him to join, but he didn't want to relocate. So Ulrich and Hetfield took the mountain to Cliff, and moved up to the Bay Area. Little did they know that they would subsequently be toasted as godfathers of the 'Bay Area thrash metal scene', spawning bands like Testament, Vio-lence and Death Angel.

Kirk, who started learning guitar when he was fifteen and took lessons from renowned guitar god Joe Satriani, first saw Metallica when his band Exodus supported them at a local show.

'This was when I hadn't heard of Metallica,' he recalls. 'No one had. It was their second gig in San Francisco, but I was just amazed at how good and how original they were. I didn't think the guitar player [Mustaine] was so hot, though. He looked a bit obnoxious.

'We ended up playing together again at a benefit gig, and I started talking to Lars backstage about the NWOBHM. I remember he undressed and got naked while we were talking. He had no inhibitions, y'know? Little did I know that it would be the first in a long series of such behaviour!'

Metallica soon left for New York, to meet up with Megaforce Records supremo Johnny Zazula (or 'Z' as he was known) who had been excited by their 'No Life T'il Leather' demo. It didn't take long for Lars, James and Cliff to decide that their guitarist had to go. Dave's drinking was getting out of control. He left, and went on to form Megadeth.

Kirk: 'When I got the call, about a month later, it was April Fools' Day, so I thought it was a joke. But then they sent me a tape of songs...'

The guitarist learned eleven tracks in a week, then scraped up enough money for a flight to New York. His former bandmates in Exodus were mightily annoyed, but it was something he had to try. He caught up with the three remaining Metallimen in a little rehearsal place in Jamaica and Queens.

'It was a complete dump. No heat, no hot water. Everyone was in sleeping bags on cardboard. I thought, "Hmmm, interesting." They were only just waking up at seven at night, so I could tell they weren't much different to me!'

The similarities continued when the four started jamming. The classic Ulrich–Hetfield–Burton–Hammett line-up was cemented, right there and then.

'They were impressed that I knew the songs really well,' says Kirk. 'I remember thinking how weird the bass player was. I had actually seen Cliff in a band called Easy Street with Jim Martin [who went on to join and eventually leave Faith No More], playing covers back in 1980. Cliff's amp blew up during that show, so he just sat in front of his amp and headbanged.'

Lars and James were grinning at each other as Kirk auditioned, intimidating the guitarist somewhat, but they were only delighted because it all felt so right.

The new Metallica soon became a finely honed metal machine. Within weeks of Kirk joining, they started recording their first album. While the original title was *Metal Up Your Ass*, complete with ludicrous artwork, they finally settled for the marginally more subtle *Kill 'Em All*.

It remains a harshly relentless album, but back then it sounded impossibly so. It was a true groundbreaker, introducing a new sound to the rock world. Roughly muted chords, wired to a satanic distortion pedal; a raucous chugging that came to be labelled 'the Bay Area crunch'. The term 'thrash metal' was also coined around this time.

'The chemistry was so much more inspirational in Metallica than it had been in Exodus,' bubbles Kirk. 'I thought Metallica was great, and I totally lived for it,

Heavier than thou Metallica on stage

even when no one bought *Kill 'Em All*. It sold, like, thirty thousand albums, which I thought was success. I never thought we'd go to a much bigger level, but then we toured and people were rabid for us.'

Metallica toured America in support of Raven.

'We had a great time,' glows Kirk. 'For the first time, we were a rock 'n' roll band on tour in the States! I was twenty years old. We were getting drunk every night, playing great shows. There were girls...the whole thing. We didn't know any better so we loved it. By the time we got to San Francisco it was amazing. The electricity onstage was so intense, and Raven were so fuckin' pissed off when they saw how well we went down in front of our hometown audience.'

Jason Newsted

Metallica then played their first European shows with their heroes Venom, gaining confidence with every fresh victory, and every compliment babbled at them by sweaty, bleeding fans. Not to mention every swig of their favourite tipple, Absolut vodka.

They were already preparing their second album, which came to be called *Ride the Lightning*. Although many of the songs were just as brutal as the *Kill...* material, it came as a surprise to many that a borderline ballad was nestling in amongst the ultraviolence.

'"Fade To Black" was one of the last songs we wrote, in an East Coast basement,' recalls Kirk. 'James had the chord progression, I had the end bit, and it all came together really well. We were into it, because it was just something different. I can remember all of us smirking and saying, "Now we have a ballad! Let's see what everyone says..."'

Metallica recorded *Ride the Lightning* in Copenhagen with producer Flemming Rasmussen, over the course of two months. On its completion, they played some European shows, then toured America again, supporting W.A.S.P. and Armored Saint.

Lars Ulrich

'It was the first time we ever had a tour bus. We thought we were kings, and we were blowing W.A.S.P. off the goddamn stage every night. The set was paced better, because we slowed it down a bit on *Ride...* with songs like, "For Whom the Bell Tolls", "Fade to Black" and "Ride the Lightning", then sped it up with "Fight Fire With Fire". But some people were already calling us sell-outs, because we had a ballad on there,' he laughs.

'We thought we were kings, and we were blowing W.A.S.P. off the goddamn stage every night.'

Cliff Burton

It's one of my favourite albums we've done. We had so much fun, or at least Cliff and I did, because we'd just sit there and play poker all night, while we were waiting for Lars to get a fucking drum sound. But the material was so great and so consistent. We were very much a product of our times. That kind of music was starting to get really popular, and rearing its head in the mainstream media. Bands like us, Anthrax and Slayer were getting written about in magazines like *Rolling Stone*.'

Around this time, Metallica changed management. It was goodbye to Johnny Z and Megaforce, and hello to Q-Prime (the bigtime management home of many a major rock band) and Elektra Records.

'It was funny,' says Kirk, 'Because me and Lars once went into record stores and joked about our albums having "Managed by Q-Prime: Peter Mensch and Cliff Burnstein" written on them. Then, all of a sudden I got a call from [*Kerrang!* journalist] Xavier Russell saying that Peter Mensch was interested. That's basically how things got rolling.'

Next up was Metallica's first headline tour of Europe. They played Britain's Donington Festival for the first time in the summer ('the biggest crowd we'd played to'). Then it was back to San Francisco, to start work on the third album, *Master of Puppets*.

'That took a while. The theory was to go straight to Denmark again and bash it out. But it took six months, which is a long time compared to the first two albums, but short compared to now.

With a title and artwork themed around both drug addiction and being a soldier at war, *Master of Puppets* remains a classic metal album. Metallica were now a band for people who wanted to like the heavier stuff, but couldn't find a tune in Slayer's *Reign In Blood*, also released that year. *Master...* had more than enough thrashing to keep the headbangers happy, while ensuring that it all found a place in the brain. "Battery" and "Damage Inc" are two of the finest assaults on the ears yet to be mounted by a so-called thrash metal band.

Then there was the classic 'Welcome Home (Sanitarium)', offering more in the way of subtlety. A dark tale of a malcontent among the maladjusted, it saw Hetfield yelling, 'Just leave me alone!', before it all went ferociously up-tempo. A whole generation of fists clenched in poster-splattered bedrooms across the world.

With a killer album like this under their bullet-belts, it was hardly surprising that Metallica landed the support slot on Ozzy Osbourne's U.S. arena tour.

'It was the first tour that really gave us a higher profile,' notes Kirk. 'We were playing to about 10,000 people a night, and building up a ton of momentum. We were very young, and fuckin' wild! It set a precedent for a few years...'

Sadly, tragedy lay in wait for Metallica. After the Ozzy tour, they hit Europe for a major headline jaunt with Anthrax in support. Just over a week into it, on 27 September, Cliff Burton was killed outright in a bus crash, as the band were approaching Copenhagen. Rock magazines of the world were filled with tributes from disbelieving fans. Nobody could quite comprehend the loss.

'Even now, I still think of Cliff every single fucking day,' says Kirk. 'I think of weird, strange things, like hearing songs that he loved. Or how he used to comb his hair...'

It was not Metallica's way, however, to break down in public and spend months telling journalists how wonderful Cliff was. They decided to stay busy.

'We were very distraught, but Cliff would have wanted us to continue. So we held auditions, which were really difficult for us, because it was only three weeks after the crash. James and I just drank and drank the whole time, and it was hard for anyone who tried out for us. Only our roadies would talk to the people we auditioned.'

This awkward process lasted a fortnight, with each candidate attempting 'Ride the Lightning', 'Fade to Black' and 'Master of Puppets'. One of the last to apply was Jason Newsted, bassist with Arizona thrashers Flotsam And Jetsam.

Cliff Burton on the Master of Puppets tour

'He said, "Okay, I know these three songs, and here's a list of twenty other songs I know," ' laughs Kirk. 'He also came with recommendations from people we knew in the business. He played most of the songs wrong, but the attitude was there and he seemed like a nice guy.

'Afterwards, we went out to a restaurant to see if we could hang with him. Me, James and Lars had a meeting in the bathroom and decided Jason was the guy. We told him, and he let out a little howl! So he was in, and all the fun began again. It was great, because we felt like a band once more.

'We wound Jason up a lot, though, because he had walked into a dream situation. Boy, did we wind him up! We'd do things like charge everything to his hotel room, and tell him that the mini bars were free. We told everyone he was gay, too. Great stuff.'

Metallica toured Japan, and then recorded a stopgap mini album, the *Garage Days Revisited* EP. Deliberately sounding sandpaper-rough, it featured covers of songs by relatively obscure bands like Budgie and the Misfits.

'That was a good way for us to break Jason in, studio-wise, before we went into a full production. We did it in a week or something, and we're really happy about that. It was the quickest we ever made an album, and it still works now. A nice little chunk of music that's not too serious.'

A detrimentally jet-lagged Metallica played their second Donington show in 1987, around the time that *Garage Days...* was released. Next up was a home video entitled *Cliff 'Em All*, released in April 1988.

'It's exactly how it looks,' says Kirk. 'Us sitting in a room getting drunk, talking about Cliff. It's not like we're putting on eulogies or anything like that. It was just happy remembrances of Cliff – a tribute, but not overly sentimental. We're heartless bastards, really!'

Album number four, *...And Justice For All*, followed. It was Metallica's most ambitious project, full of epic tracks using a multitude of different sections and ideas.

'It was definitely on the progressive side of things. We were trying to tell the world that we were musicians, because at the time that was very much the vogue. Solo guitarists were making albums that went gold and platinum. We kinda got caught up in that whole virtuosity thing.

'We had some kind of vision as to how it would sound, but...I don't know. It just didn't happen. When Jason first heard a tape of the mix, he walked off the bus, because there was so little bass on there. He hadn't been in the band long enough to really assert himself. I felt bad for him, but I was caught up in my own lead stuff being loud enough! In retrospect, the songs are great, but the sound isn't close to anything we'd do now.'

James Hetfield

The best-known track is 'One' – the first song that the previously MTV-resistant Metallica made a promo video for, and the tune which cemented the band's crossover appeal. Whether you liked the music or not, you could understand the torment of a paralysed soldier trapped in his own head. The song was inspired by a film based on the Dalton Trumbo book *Johnny's Got His Gun*, and Metallica's powerful video used clips from the movie to considerably unsettling effect. It also took the unprecedented step of having dialogue occasionally dominate the music in the mix.

'Nowadays, you see a lot of videos like that,' Kirk points out. 'I remember seeing the final copy of the video and being in awe. America still didn't play us on the radio, but that video got a lot of airplay on MTV. I knew we'd struck a chord when I saw "One" played one night, and afterwards the VJ said, "Whoah! Okay, on a lighter note, here's Michael Jackson..."'

Kirk: 'We had made it to the next level, which was arena rock. We wanted to see if we could put on a real show. That kinda set the tone for the next tour, with the diamond-shaped stage and the snakepit.'

Jason Newsted

As the resulting tour progressed, the band realised how excessively long some of this new material was.

'I liked playing the song "...And Justice For All", for about the first four or five months of the tour,' laughs Kirk. 'Then it suddenly hit me one night, and I thought, "God, this song is long. If it wasn't for the big fuckin' bang at the end, people would be walking out."'

Metallica had a major stage set, complete with Lady Justice statue which collapsed on cue, and a massive lighting rig.

Kirk: 'We had made it to the next level, which was arena rock. We wanted to see if we could put on a real show. That kinda set the tone for the next tour, with the diamond-shaped stage and the snakepit.'

This brings us to the multi-million selling *Metallica* album, released in August 1991. The album's recording/mixing marathon saw tension between the band and their new producer. Bob Rock had handled many a big-seller for mainstream rock bands like Bon Jovi and Mötley Crüe.

'The making of that album was strange,' says Kirk, 'because it was the first time we had ever truly worked with a producer. Flemming Rasmussen was more of an engineer than anything, and his ideas weren't so song-oriented as Bob's. Bob was also a musician, so he could contribute ideas about minor chords or whatever.

'At first, we didn't want to give in to a lot of his ideas. I felt, "Who is this guy, trying to tell us how to play our instruments?" He also felt he had to prove something to us. We clashed a lot, but I definitely think it helped the music.'

The album is indeed a powerful, exquisitively crafted beast, but it had a certain portion of ex-fans shouting 'Sell out!' from the rooftops.

'That's because it was so accessible and easy to get on first listen,' defends Kirk. 'That's not our fault. It's just a product of good songwriting, playing and production. We did a good job, and a lot of people saw that as commercial. But like I said, some people saw *Ride the Lightning* that way!

'Our attitude was that we'd already done really aggressive stuff like "Damage Inc". People will argue with us until the cows come home, but we just didn't want to stay with the same formula.'

Untouched by the domination of 'grunge' bands like Nirvana and Pearl Jam elsewhere, the *Metallica* tour lasted two and a half years. Full details could probably fill this chapter alone.

'It went on for ever, because that album went on for ever!' laughs Kirk. 'We sold albums everywhere, and the demand for us to play was everywhere. The album was so huge in the States that we went to certain markets three times. We went to Europe three times.

James Hetfield

Jason Newsted

'The stage set was great,' he chuckles. 'It was like running around a playground, except you had a guitar strapped to you.'

Of course, filling arenas every night invariably leads to egomaniacal rock star antics. It's well documented that Lars was by far the worst offender, but Kirk is ready to defend him.

'When you get so much attention, you have to assume some sort of role, just to be able to deal with everything. All of us had so much pressure, and sometimes you do that stuff, just to be able to adjust to everything. I think that was part of it. I didn't give Lars as much shit for his white leather jacket as the other guys – I just didn't think it was aesthetically a good idea!

'It got to a point where we were all pretty distant from each other, due to the demands and the pressure. You get caught up in it, and you know it will pass. It's not a permanent thing – it's just what happens when you're on tour. Luckily, we had enough experience to understand that, and give each other space.'

An early highlight of the tour came when Metallica appeared at the Freddie Mercury Tribute Concert at Wembley Stadium, playing a three-song set. James realised a childhood dream by singing Queen's 'Stone Cold Crazy' with the remaining members of Queen and Black Sabbath guitarist Tony Iommi.

Matters then took an intriguing turn in the summer of 1992, when Metallica embarked on a co-headlining trek across America with multi-platinum rockers Guns N'Roses. It seemed like a good idea, until disagreements cropped up between the two bands.

'It really showed us who or what we didn't want to turn into,' Kirk sighs. 'It was apples and oranges, and Guns weren't as professional as we were. Axl started acting up about things here and there, starting rows with Lars. At the end it became a big soap opera, especially when James got burnt...'

This happened in Montreal on 8 August, when a pyro exploded prematurely during 'Fade to Black'.

Kirk: 'I was playing the intro solo, and James' guitar dropped out. Then I saw Lars wasn't at his drumkit, so I ran backstage and saw these techs

'The stage set was great,' he chuckles. 'It was like running around a playground, except you had a guitar strapped to you.'

pouring water over James. I saw the skin on his hand raise and blister. He was in shock. Then Axl didn't want to be outdone, so he walked off stage himself. Then a riot happened, and I almost had a nervous breakdown. We were trapped in the arena, and I remember Axl saying, "The kids outside are turning over cop cars. Cool!" I just looked at him and thought, "Man, this guy really doesn't get it." '

For a few weeks, Metallica were joined by Metal Church guitarist John Marshall, allowing Hetfield merely to sing.

Looking back, Kirk admits that the epic *Metallica* tour, 'Fucking killed us. By the end I was really torn, because I was so accustomed to lacking any foundation. I felt disjointed because I didn't have one spot to always go back to. But at the same time, I was so tired of the other guys. I was afraid of domestic life again, but I had to get away from them.'

Kirk eased his post-tour depression by going back to school and taking Film, Jazz and Asian studies. Still, the band's work had reaped great rewards. *Metallica* sold more than all its predecessors combined, and yielded numerous hit singles including 'The Unforgiven' and the soul-baring 'Nothing Else Matters'. The first, 'Enter Sandman', became that once-in-a-generation rarity – the song that salesmen in guitar shops are sick of hearing prospective buyers attempt to play, just like Led Zeppelin's 'Stairway to Heaven'.

The tour bug struck Metallica again the following year, however, when they embarked on the *Shit Hits the Sheds* Summer tour across America, playing smaller arenas than before.

'That was more to jump-start our creative process and practise our chops,' says Kirk. 'It was also my moment where I felt like I'd drifted away from the other guys. I was into a lot of bad stuff. Drugs, drink. I had a bad relationship, so I kinda alienated the guys for a while. By the end, though, I came back to earth and we had a great time.'

The next task was to write new material, and this, predictably, took six months. Metallica then began recording the album which would eventually bear the title *Load* – interrupting the process only to headline Donington, and play a festival in the Arctic Circle.

Kirk: 'We realised we had a lot of material. I had, like, ninety-one pieces of music or something, because the last tour was so damn long. That's why we've still got twelve songs that aren't recorded from that writing session.'

Another once in a generation riff from Hetfield

'It was fine,' Kirk laughs. 'No bolts of lightning came down and struck us for playing Lollapolooza at all! It turned out that two-thirds of the people had seen us before anyway.'

Cynics insist, of course, that Metallica have become the kind of classic rock band that they originally wanted to seek and destroy.

Kirk Hammett shakes his head. 'We were never out to destroy anyone. We were just out to make our mark. It's very immature, to think that way. It's all about writing the music you want to write, and expressing yourself however you like. All that other stuff doesn't make a difference any more...'

Nothing else matters, indeed.

Load caught Metallica in a more laidback, if not more commercial, frame of mind. They loosened their trademark mechanical style, sounding closer to 'classic rock' than ever. This shocked many, as did the band's new short haircuts.

'*Load* might not be as extreme as our previous albums, but we wanted it to be a certain way,' explains Kirk. 'We picked songs that fitted well with each other, and it just so happened they weren't as extreme as the others. The next album should rock harder, and it will hopefully be out at the end of '97.'

In the summer of 1996, Metallica caused minor controversy by headlining the Lollapolooza festival, a traditionally 'alternative' affair. However, with bands like Green Day and Pearl Jam having become the mainstream, the word 'alternative' probably applied better to Metallica than anyone else.

KIRK HAMMETT

Favourite album: I'd have to say *Electric Ladyland*, Jimi Hendrix. I first heard that album when I was seven years old. It took me a while to fully understand it, though.

First gig attended: It was either Thin Lizzy or Robin Trower. I think it was Thin Lizzy in '77, and it totally changed my life. I could not believe that the people I stared at on album sleeves for hours and hours were actually in the same room with me.

Motto for a successful life: Buy more guitars! Get your chin pierced!

Most embarrassing tour story: I have quite a few of those, but I can never remember them! Let's see. One would be a certain Ross Halfin taking pictures of me naked – not thinking that he would print them. Lo and behold, there I was in *Kerrang!* I was pissed off, but I laugh at it now.

Favourite food: Sushi. I love sushi. Mexican food, too. I like a good dose of pasta there, too.

ALBUM DISCOGRAPHY:

Kill 'Em All (1983)

Ride the Lightning (1984)

Master of Puppets (1986)

The $5.98 Garage Days Revisited EP (1987)

...And Justice For All (1988)

Metallica (1991)

Load (1996)

My favourite recipe is for a good dry martini. Bombay Sapphire gin, with maybe the slightest hint of extra dry vermouth, and two olives. Shaken, not stirred.

Hobbies: I'm into horror movies and memorabilia. My favourite horror movie would be *The Mummy*, from 1933. I also like *The Evil Dead*, *Hellraiser*, *Francis Ford Coppola's Dracula* and tons of stuff. I also mountainbike and smoke enormous cigars quite a bit. I like gambling – does that count?'

Causes supported: I'm pro-choice. I support all outreach programmes, especially for the homeless or people who are HIV positive.

What would surprise someone most about you? I'm really open-minded, and a little bit off my rocker and wild. A lot of people see me as quiet and soft-spoken, and I am when it comes to business, but after all the business is done with, I'm a little bit nuts. I'll try just about anything.

If your house was burning, what would you save first? Pictures of my friends and relatives. And my cats. How much luggage space do I have? Because then I'd take all the band memorabilia, my guitars, and my horror movie collection!

Dark and introspective Metallica in the late nineties

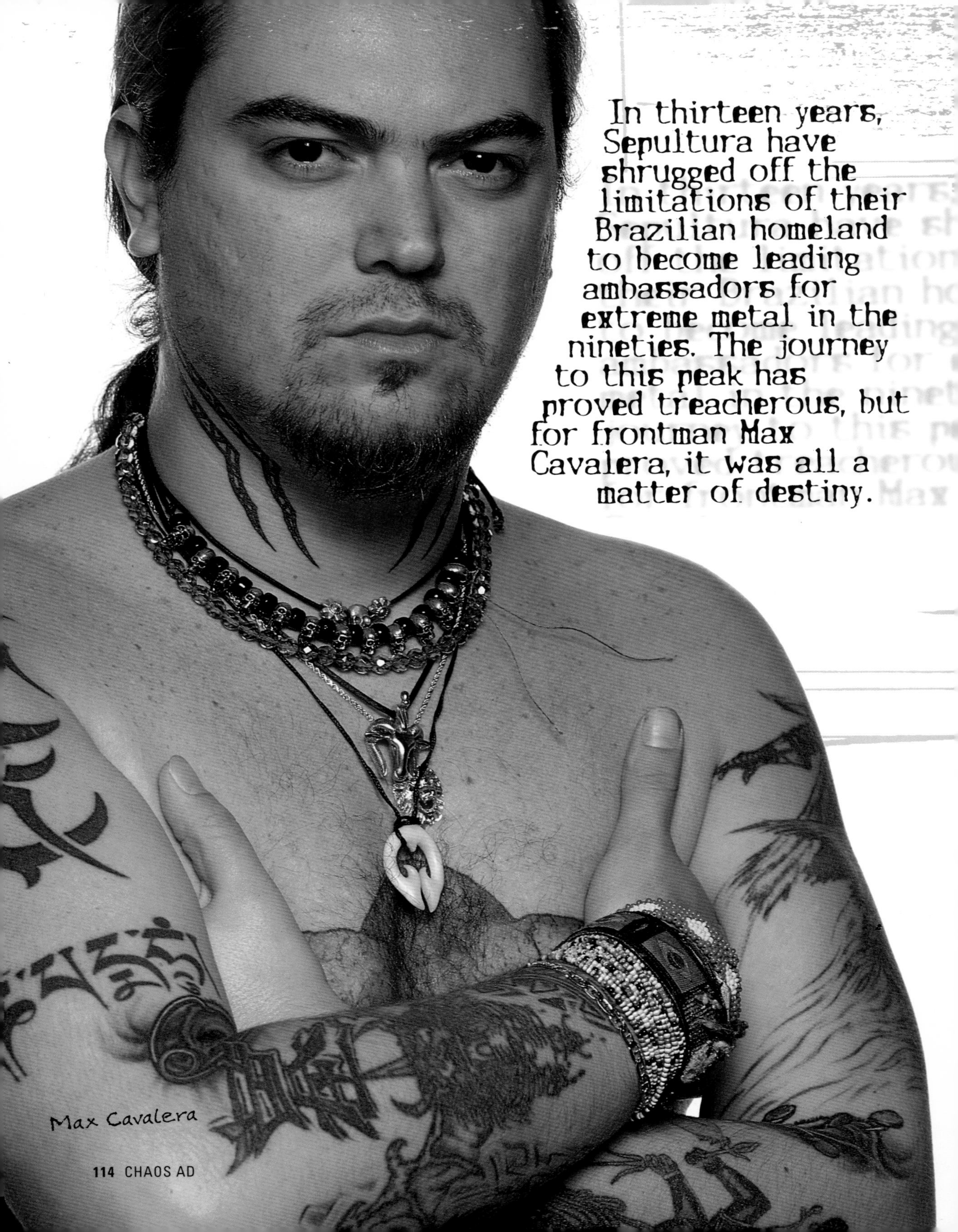

In thirteen years, Sepultura have shrugged off the limitations of their Brazilian homeland to become leading ambassadors for extreme metal in the nineties. The journey to this peak has proved treacherous, but for frontman Max Cavalera, it was all a matter of destiny.

Max Cavalera

SEPULTURA

'My goal as a kid was to go ahead and get my father's job at the Italian Embassy,' he recalls. 'Now, I think I understand why he died. It was all meant to be that way. Sepultura would never have existed otherwise. I would never have had all this hate inside me.'

As Metallica began smoothing down the commercially limiting spikes of their sound, in the late eighties and early nineties, a super-hungry Sepultura were reaching a new level of intensity. *Beneath the Remains* is seen by many as Sepultura's truly classic contribution to the thrash metal genre – when it emerged in 1989, it was as if the rock media had been plugged into the National Grid.

Extreme music had been relatively stagnant for a few years. The last classic releases had been Slayer's *Reign In Blood* and Metallica's *Master of Puppets* in 1986. Indeed, the more devout followers of hard sounds might even contest that the latter is a classic.

Suddenly, along came four Brazilian pups, unleashing a speedball of manic energy and giving complacent thrashers a good kick in the shorts. *Beneath the Remains* was heavy yet supremely tight. It was seriously aggressive, yet not without the odd moment of warped melody. It was that rarity in the genre – an album made by strong musicians, with imagination.

Because it was the band's first worldwide release, many saw it as their debut, when in fact it was their third full-length album. But Sepultura had been together since 1984, struggling to get on. It's encouraging indeed that this band, whose music is so driven by no-holds-barred aggression, should go on to sell millions of albums worldwide. One reason has to be their overwhelming authenticity. There's history here.

While so many hard-edged bands can only pretend that their music is inspired by similarly hard times in their personal lives, Sepultura can tell you some stories you will never forget. Life may be easier now for them, but it never used to be. Max Cavalera (vocals/guitar), his brother Igor (drums), Andreas Kisser (guitar) and bassman Paulo Jr will never forget that. Why do you expect they called their most recent, sixth album *Roots*?

Max and Igor were born in Belo Horizonte into a relatively affluent family, with an Italian father who worked at the Italian Embassy. They spent most of their early childhood in São Paulo.

'We were living in a really nice, middle-class type situation, almost moving on into upper class,' admits Max. 'Everything was like a perfect childhood. We'd go to soccer games and embassy parties, stuff like that.'

It was in 1979, however, that the Cavaleras' comfortable lifestyle was to collapse. Max and Igor's father died, after a frighteningly sudden heart attack.

'There had been no sign of anything like that before,' says Max. 'One day, he was just out. Gone. The thing is, he never left anything to us. He was never prepared to die, so the only money he left was a contribution that the embassy gives to families after any member dies.

'That was a real shock. I was nine years old and Igor was eight. But for me it was more drastic because my father died in my arms. It was hard to get over that. I still haven't got over it, and I don't think I ever will. With Zyon [Max's elder son] and everything now, it's better, but those demons will always be with me.'

The Cavaleras moved back to Belo Horizonte and Max describes the following year as 'real crazy'.

'We lost the good life. We were used to stuff like buying new soccer balls and clothes. Next thing, we were wearing clothes that were passed on to us by our grandmother and stuff! My mom needed money, so me and Igor went to work right away. We made ice cream in the house, then put it in a box and sold it around the neighbourhood.'

The Cavaleras' mother didn't know what to do with her boys, and so finally sent them to a military school named Tira Dentes. From her point of view, it turned out to be a terrible idea. From the point of view of millions of future Sepultura fans, it was the best thing she could have done. Military school got the brothers into metal music and taught them how to be rebellious. Fantastic.

Soon, the name *Trops De Choque* started appearing in their school books, where their homework should have been. It meant Shock Troops, and it was the name of the band which the teenagers wished they were in.

Then *Sepultura* appeared. The word means 'grave' in Portuguese, and they plucked this notion from the Motorhead song 'Dancing On Your Grave'.

At military school, the brothers met the man who would eventually become their first singer. Wagner Lamounier was an out-of-control rebel who led the Cavaleras on such foolish nocturnal missions as robbing skulls from graveyards, before dropping them on a highway.

Igor Cavalera

'He was like us, but totally pissed off and fucked up,' recalls Max. 'He was a little bit crazier than us, and we totally connected to him right away. His father was a military guy, though, which was strange. He lived in a great area of Belo Horizonte, and I still don't understand why he was such a rebel...

'I think that because our family had everything, then lost it, it makes me appreciate everything that comes. I never take anything for granted. If something like Donington happens, or a gold album, it really means a lot.'

So the Cavaleras carried on scribbling band logos and lyrics in their school books, while getting off on hard-to-find bootleg recordings of bands like the Sex Pistols, Motorhead and the Swiss dukes of discord, Hellhammer.

'I lost my mind when I heard Punk,' marvels Max. 'I didn't know what was metal any more, but I knew I loved it all.'

The Cavaleras and Wagner were finally possessed by the urge to turn this entity called Sepultura into a band, after attending a free festival headlined by thrashers Dorsal Atlantica.

Max: 'It was like a small version of Woodstock with about 5,000 people. We were also forced to travel with all kinds of crazy people and some chickens for the forty-hour bus ride from Belo. Some people think touring in a van is punk, but that's luxury, man!'

The baaad onstage attitude of Dorsal's frontman especially raised Max's eyebrows high.

'The first thing the guy said into the microphone was, "Alright, we're Dorsal Atlantica. I hate jocks and playboy people! If there are any of those fuckers here, I'll be waiting after the show to beat the shit out of them!"

'I thought it was God!' he exclaims. And while Max has never been this offensive to his audience, it's a surefire bet that Sepultura's overflow of attitude was stoked there and then.

The Cavaleras were subsequently moved from military school to Dom Cabral – a religious school. Great idea.

'We'd have Venom's "Black Metal" T-shirts on under our religious school uniform!' laughs Max. 'That was nice. We always got into trouble there, too. But it was only a year. After that, we were gone. It didn't work at all, and it was actually worse than the military school.'

Not that Max and Igor were worried about their lack of academic achievements. They now had a band, and were having great fun making a load of primitive noise. In turn, their mother knew it was keeping them off the dangerous streets.

Max: 'A lot of people we knew were dealing drugs, stealing or whatever. We also had friends who were fucking girls or other guys for money. So music was our choice, even though we were poor and fucked up from the beginning. But from every gig we got a little more money, and the Cogumelo deal helped towards equipment and the house.'

Max Cavalera

Sepultura l r Igor Cavalera Andreas Kisser Paulo Jr Max Cavalera

The first ever Sepultura gig took place in Belo in December 1984. They supported fellow-countrymen Overdose in a dive called Barroliche. Sepultura's holocaustic assault still lacked a bass guitar. They neither knew nor cared.

Laughs Max: 'We didn't find out that we needed a bass until later. It was really noisy, man, and only three drunk Motorhead fans enjoyed it. The thing that I remember most about that first show was that my guitar was completely out of tune. Not even one note was slightly in. The gig was shit.'

Sepultura eventually wised up to their need for a bassist, enlisting Roberto 'The Cat', although no one ever seemed to know the origin of this nickname. They began rehearsing in The Cat's garage but this arrangement was shortlived because Paulo Jr was destined to enter the frame. Returning from his school holidays, he heard a Sepultura rehearsal tape. And hated it. But still, a friend persuaded him to come down to see the band play in a garage, and he was greatly amused by Igor's incredibly basic kit, utilising plant stands and a broom.

Paulo ended up replacing Roberto, mainly due to the fact that he actually owned a bass, and didn't have to borrow one for each rehearsal. The new Sepultura line-up continued to gig and slowly accrue experience, although when relations with Wagner collapsed Max finally surprised the others with a decision.

'One day out of the blue I thought, "Fuck it, I'm gonna sing,"' he says. 'Wagner came to practice one day, all excited. But I grabbed his bag and threw it on the floor. I said, "You'd better go now. You're fired." He was very pissed off, and it was a bad split.'

But a fateful one. The destiny factor again. Who could imagine Sepultura today without Max roaring hell into the microphone?

People were flocking in rising numbers to see Sepultura (by now featuring Jairo T on guitar), and the band finally accepted a recording offer from Cogumelo Records. The label also ran a metal-oriented record shop, which Sepultura unsurprisingly hung around like bees in honey, and it was a counter assistant there who nudged Cogumelo in Sepultura's direction.

The label paid for them to record a demo track, 'Necromancer'. Max likens that first ever studio experience to 'walking on to a spaceship! When "Necromancer" was done, I just listened to it over and over again. By this time we were listening to a lot of European thrash bands, like Kreator and Destruction. The demo wasn't as good quality-wise as those, but it was still comparable to Hellhammer and Venom. It was ugly enough, and we couldn't wait to put the other songs down.'

They did, and the result was 1985's *Bestial Devastation* – Sepultura's half of a split LP with Overdose. The sound might have been rougher than sandpaper on a hedgehog's back, but Sepultura sounded hungry. Not to mention downright satanic.

'People who heard the album couldn't believe we were from Belo,' Max remembers. 'They thought we were from Germany, like Kreator or something. It was great, although Overdose got better reviews because their sound was so perfect. They'd been together practising for five years, and we'd been together for about one!'

Sepultura would load up with boxes of the albums, take the nine-hour ride to São Paulo, and sell them on the streets. Eventually, they shifted more than a thousand.

In 1986, the band ended up recording their debut album, *Morbid Visions*, in São Paulo. This was the equivalent of a band from smalltown America going to record in Los Angeles. Having said that, they were forced to stay at Paulo's aunt's house, surviving on one meal a day.

Max: 'Cogumelo put more money into *Morbid Visions*, letting us record in a big studio. But *Morbid Visions* ended up sounding like shit! *Bestial Devastation* sounds better!

'I don't know what went wrong. I think we were just so excited about recording our first full-length album that we just went crazy! We used too many effects, especially on the vocals and the snare. I sound like I'm singing in a tunnel!'

Nevertheless, it led to Sepultura fulfilling long-held dreams of playing with Venom, which they did in Belo, even if meeting the Geordie metallers proved disappointing.

'We thought they'd be so fucking cool,' says Max, 'but they came in Spandex pants, with a total attitude. We tried to say hello to them in the lobby and they told us to get the fuck out of there! Our idols just fell apart in front of our eyes...'

Spurred on by this, Sepultura promptly stole the show. The next event on their calendar was swapping the increasingly blues-obsessed Jairo T for São Paulo man Andreas Kisser. Andreas, ironically enough, was Max's guitar-tech on the last show with Jairo.

Andreas introduced a new sonic dimension to Sepultura. He started this process by forcefeeding Metallica's *Master of Puppets* to Max.

Max: 'I used to think it was commercial crap, but decided it was actually pretty good. I didn't like the ballads but stuff like "Battery" was great. So Andreas opened up a whole new door for us, and that's why the *Schizophrenia* album was so different from *Morbid Visions*. A real turning point...'

Schizophrenia was released in 1987. One of the first examples of vicious death metal finding time to incorporate the odd melody, it soon blazed a trail by word-of-mouth through the musical underworld. The grapevine started twitching, then violently shaking.

While worldwide fanzines began tripping over themselves to make contact (Max having to communicate via a translator), Sepultura went on to make history by supporting punk band RDP at Brazil's first-ever metal/punk show. Before, promoters lined up strictly one or the other.

'He gave me a free ticket,' smiles Max, 'to fly from Belo to New York, stay for two days and come back. I had to pretend to be a PanAm employee. In exchange for the ticket, I gave him a bunch of Sepultura videos to sell in Brazil...'

In a comic scene, Max arrived at JFK airport in a suit and tie, with his hair slicked back. As soon as he got out of the airport, however, he put his Possessed shirt on.

During these two adrenalin-pumping days, Max stayed at a 'dump' in Manhattan. 'There were cockroaches on the walls, but I didn't care,' he shrugs. 'It was great! We went to all the labels, like Combat and Roadrunner. Nobody really responded enthusiastically, though, so I came home a little bummed out. I was happy to have been in America for the first time, but I also doubted that anyone would sign us.'

These doubts continued for about a month, until destiny finally got on the phone. The voice on the crackly line was Roadrunner Records' A&R supremo Monte Conner.

Max: 'He said he wanted more details on Sepultura, because he wanted to sign us. We were doing fucking backflips, man, we were so excited!'

'Only one hundred people showed up in a place that held six,' spits Max. 'Five hundred people knew about the show, which was supposed to be a sell-out, but they were too fucking scared to come. The skinheads showed up but the promoter came outside and chased them all away! He was a really crazy guy.'

Now that Sepultura were playing over twenty gigs a year (not many by today's standards, but plenty in Brazil), Cogumelo could no longer hold them. Max sent copies of *Schizophrenia* to various labels and radio stations in the States. The feedback was so positive that Max knew he had to go to New York and push his band. But how?

In March 1988, destiny called once again. Max had a friend who worked for PanAm Airways...

Sepultura signed and returned the contract through the post, then holed up in Paulo's house for days on end, intensively writing new material for what eventually became *Beneath the Remains*. They recorded it with an American producer, Scott Burns, in Rio De Janeiro.

Max: 'The way the album was received was the biggest surprise of all. It took Europe by storm, if I remember. I can't think of anything exactly like that since. Maybe Machine Head's *Burn My Eyes*...'

In September, the quartet arrived in Europe for the first time. Supporting German thrashers Sodom, they hacked and slashed their way through fifty-two gigs, leaving jaws on the floor to be scraped up. The intensity level was verging on the ridiculous.

'We're not really moving away from death metal,' he told interviewers who asked. 'We're just trying to find our style. *Bestial Devastation* and *Morbid Visions* ripped other bands off, but the new stuff's Sepultura music.'

A rampage through America followed, to almost unanimous acclaim. Sepultura had arrived, and it was 1991 before they recorded the follow-up to *Beneath...*, which many people saw as their debut.

Written in a Brazilian rehearsal space co-populated by heroin junkies, and beset by pressure and the odd problem of excess in the Seps' camp, *Arise* is generally seen a transitional disc with some good songs.

'Pressure can sometimes make Sepultura do cool stuff,' admits Max, 'But too much fucks up the whole thing. We had a lot of pressure on our shoulders at that point – having to follow up *Beneath the Remains* – but we were too fucked up to understand that pressure. We were just going with the flow...'

Like most musicians let loose in the rock circus, Max drank like a fish and dabbled with drugs. His biggest problem was cocaine, until he met his wife and manager-to-be, Gloria Bujnowski.

Max: 'I never got to the point where I would carry it around with me myself, but I did start selling CDs to get coke. I was getting into that dangerous area. That's when I met Gloria. She's so anti hard drugs, and she was the best thing that happened to me. She explained exactly how I'd end up if I continued doing cocaine. I would sell the house, sell myself and then kill myself. That's when I got fucking scared of cocaine and I've never touched it since.'

While the *Arise* tour had some great moments like opening up the prestigious Rock In Rio II festival, Max finally saw the reality of the situation.

'If I hadn't slowed down the drinking and stopped the drugs, Sepultura wouldn't be here right now. We'd be history. It's true, man – who the fuck is gonna pay ten dollars to see a bunch of shit? Face it, it's a jungle out there, and everyone's doing the best they can. Now, I just feed on adrenalin, and I'm more worried about playing well.'

The *Arise* tour never seemed to end. Sepultura toured with Ozzy Osbourne (including two Black Sabbath reunion shows in Costa Mesa), and then Ministry. The album went on to sell over a million copies worldwide.

Before facing the task of spawning a fifth album, Max found time to not only form Nailbomb, a hugely heavy side-project band with Alex Newport from Nottingham noisemakers Fudge Tunnel, but create little Zyon Cavalera with wife and manager Gloria. Zyon's heartbeat was sampled *in utero*, and can be heard at the outset of the subsequent 1993 Seps album, *Chaos AD*.

Chaos... saw Sepultura really let loose, and draw away from the more clinical approach of *Arise*. Chaos reigned supreme, with lethal results. The first single, 'Territory', infiltrated the UK Top Seventy-five for the first time, at Number 66. The album hit the national charts at Number 11.

These achievements were momentarily clouded by the first of a few incidents that occurred during the *Chaos...* era. Returning home after a Rage Against the Machine gig in Phoenix, Arizona (where they now lived), Max, Gloria and two friends were shot at in the street. When Max retaliated, his party were, amazingly, arrested...

'I still can't understand it, really,' shrugs Max. 'It all happened very fast, but it really showed up the mentality of jocks and rednecks in Phoenix. They didn't like long hair, tattoos or green hair. It was just territorial bullshit.'

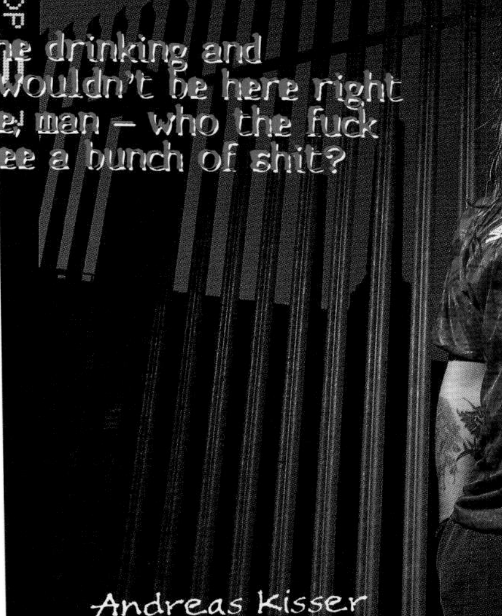

RDP

Andreas Kisser

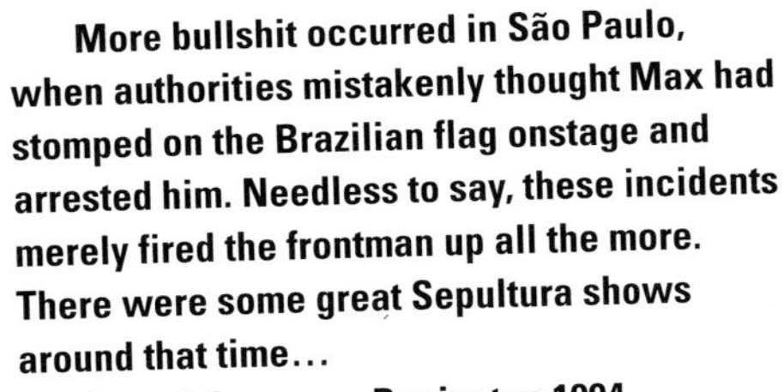

More bullshit occurred in São Paulo, when authorities mistakenly thought Max had stomped on the Brazilian flag onstage and arrested him. Needless to say, these incidents merely fired the frontman up all the more. There were some great Sepultura shows around that time...

One of them was Donington 1994, headlined by Aerosmith. Sepultura wowed the thousands not only with their vulgar display of power, but with 'Kaiowas' – the tribally percussive *Chaos...* track. The band pounded drums in unison, creating the day's most enduring image.

Sepultura spent much of 1995 writing and recording *Roots,* the sixth album. Max confirmed that the title was a reference to '*Our* roots, and not forgetting them. It's about remembering where you come from, and how you evolve and develop. Once you've lost your roots, it's over. You're not yourself any more, and you're just there with all the other shit sell-out bands. You become a musical hooker!'

Ironically recorded in the idyllic Indigo Ranch, way up in the Malibu mountains, *Roots* amply displayed that Sepultura couldn't turn to sonic prostitution if they tried. Although the speedball brain surgery of *Beneath the Remains* had been replaced by thick waves of black riffing shackled to increasingly tribal rhythms, it is probably the heaviest thing they have created. Not the fastest, but the heaviest.

This time, however, Sepultura took the concept of 'Kaiowas' one step further, enlisting Brazil's Xavante tribe to chant on the acoustic, percussive song 'Itsari'. The concept was inspirational, and achieving it was less problematic than expected.

'I personally called the president of the Tribe Culture Centre,' says Max, 'and explained to her who I was. She knew the name Sepultura. I explained the importance of this album, and the title *Roots*. She told me that a record had been made out in the jungle last year. She had the necessary stuff – an eight-track machine and an engineer.

'That was helpful, because when you really think about it, you go, "Where do you get power in the jungle?" Even I thought it might be too wild an idea, but we ended up using car batteries. We couldn't play the music back, only record stuff.

'The chief of the tribe could speak Portuguese, so that made things kind of easy. I'd tell the chief what we wanted to do, and he would explain it to the whole tribe. Everything was based around meetings, and talking about yourself. They definitely wanted you to be straight with them. They were a bit like a record company!

'They definitely had their own culture,' he says, admiringly. 'They don't look or act Brazilian. The majority of Brazilians have the reputation of being lazy and not caring about things. This tribe were the opposite – really active. I won't forget that time. I love the song, but the whole experience was really the shit.'

This mission not only silenced critics who bleated that Sepultura had turned their backs on their home country, but provided *Roots* with a hypnotically soothing piece of atmosphere.

Max finds the ferocity of album tracks like 'Straight Hate', 'Spit' and 'Attitude' easy to explain. He may be a father of two now (with Igor Amadeus Cavalera having been born during the creation of *Roots*), but his inner fires still burn strongly. 'A lot of *Roots* stuff was more personal than political. I mean every fucking line of those songs.'

Sadly, just prior to publication, the rock world was shocked to hear the news that Sepultura had split up following irreconcilable differences. Andreas, Igor and Paulo Jr will continue with the Sepultura name, Andreas taking over lead vocal duties. Max is already working on a solo album.

'I've always been on a search for the heaviest guitar sound I can get,' he smiles. 'People think I'm just insane, because I keep looking. It's in my head somewhere, but I haven't quite found it yet. I will, one of these days, and I'm gonna record it. Then, I can quit...'

Somehow, you get the feeling that destiny won't allow this.

'Once you've lost your roots, it's over. You're not yourself any more, and you're just there with all the other shit sell-out bands. You become a musical hooker!'

l r Max Cavalera, Paulo Jr, Igor Cavalera, Andreas Kisser

MAX CAVALERA

Favourite album: I would have to say Black Sabbath's *Sabotage* album (1975). It's still got the same impact today as it did when I first heard it. *Sabotage* has really got everything. Heavy stuff, weird stuff, melodic stuff. But it's hard to choose one album, because I listen to everything from Brazilian music to early Celtic Frost!

Motto for a successful life: Always go for your gut feeling and try to do things without paying attention to what other people think of you. If you have one idea, stick to it until it's done. Like when I went to New York to see record companies in 1988. It was a pioneering idea for Brazil, but it got Sepultura the record deal with Roadrunner.

Tour story: I'll try to remember one. Okay, we were playing five Christmas shows with Motorhead one year, and we were so excited about it. But they said we couldn't play our cover of their song 'Orgasmatron', even though it was really popular with our fans at that time. So when Motorhead were playing 'Orgasmatron' one night, we went on stage wearing masks that Igor made, along with half-naked roadies wearing socks on their dicks. Just like the Chili Peppers! It was really fucked up and funny, but I don't think Motorhead laughed much. Never mind, they can come on to our stage and do it any time they like!

Causes supported: There are so many that I truly believe in. The most important would be anti-racism, because I can't put up with people trying to get fascist shit back together. I'm obviously against violence towards children, and having had kids, I'm really thinking about it for the first time. People killing kids and abusing them. Those kids could have been you or me...

Favourite food: That's got to be rice and black beans. Very simple and very popular in Brazil. It's what we ate all the time when we lived there, every day. Sometime it would come with potatoes or chicken. Of course, my mom makes the best!

Hobbies: I like to play a little bit of soccer sometimes, just kicking a ball around. Something else I really enjoy doing is making compilation tapes and sending them to friends. I even make Xeroxed covers for them. I used to do it in Brazil and I never stopped. Of course, when someone shows me one of my old compilation tapes, I just laugh!

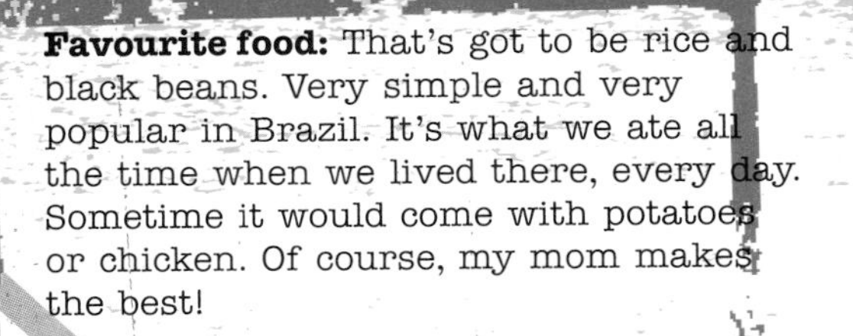

What would surprise someone most about you? The fact that I'm really religious and spiritually minded. I spend a lot of time with my personal religion, and I pray for about twenty minutes each day. Part of it comes from my mother, who used to do white voodoo stuff, mixed with stuff from Africa. Part of it comes from my beliefs in God. At the same time, I'm really against what the Church stands for.

If your house was burning, what would you save first? Once my family were out, of course, I'd probably be stupid enough to go back in and take my first guitar. It's a real old white BC Rich, all beat up, and it doesn't even play in tune any more. But it's got really strong sentimental value.

ALBUM DISCOGRAPHY:

Bestial Devastation (a split album with Overdose) (1985)
Morbid Visions (1986)
Schizophrenia (1987)
Beneath the Remains (1989)
Arise (1991)
Chaos AD (1993)
Roots (1996)

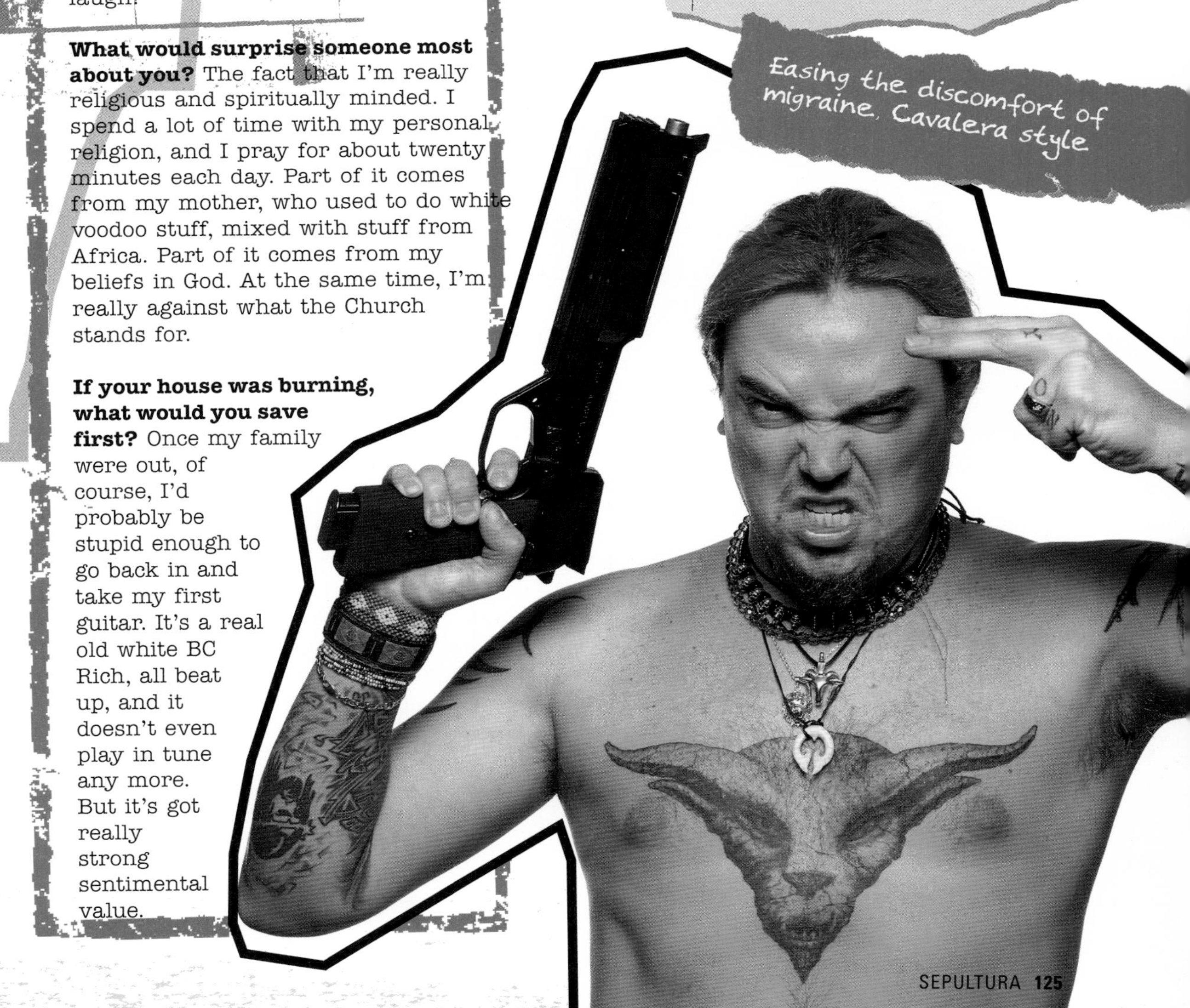

Easing the discomfort of migraine, Cavalera style

NEW BANDS FOR THE NINETIES

NINE INCH

The phenomenon of Nine Inch Nails has provided nineties rock with perhaps its most revolutionary new force. The band has the unusual distinction of being the brainchild of just one man, Michael Trent Reznor. With two albums, two mini-albums and a brace of EPs and singles to his name, Reznor has consistently rejected standard rock stereotypes in a ruthless campaign to create something completely new. Machines, synthesizers and computers have been fused with heavy guitars to engulf the listener in tidal waves of sound. In the solitude of the studio, Reznor has manufactured a kind of controlled chaos, the sound of an earthquake in hell. Almost single-handedly, he has defied the establishment, proving that what can be achieved in rock is limited solely by the scope of an artist's imagination.

Trent Reznor NIN

Born in 1965, he spent most of his childhood in Mercer, Pennsylvania. At the age of five, he went to live with his grandparents who he still regards with great fondness. Everyone always called him Trent, because his father had also been christened Michael. Although his was not an unhappy childhood, he found it difficult to fit in with other children, and became fascinated with science fiction and horror movies. He believes that seeing *The Exorcist* and *The Omen* at an early age had a detrimental effect on his mind. He became subject to paranoid fantasies, believing that the devil wanted his soul. In fear of being possessed, he would regularly check his scalp in case the mark of the devil had appeared.

The only thing Trent Reznor became possessed by was music. A love of vintage Kiss prompted him to study computer engineering and music at college. These three interests clearly show how NIN was conceived. After a series of embarrassing band projects, Reznor branched out on his own, cementing his computer skills with his music skills for the first time. The result was *Pretty Hate Machine*, Nine Inch Nails' debut album. Reznor used bleak washes of synthesizers, suddenly punctuating them with shrieking guitars and his own immense vocal power. At this time, NIN also gained a reputation for their gruelling videos, often containing controversial, sado-masochistic imagery.

Initially, the media were unsure of how to deal with the band. Were they metal, indie, or something else altogether? In the sphere of rock music, nothing like this had been heard before. The public was left to make its own decision. *Pretty Hate Machine* went on to sell 500,000 copies. The primary exponent of industrial metal had arrived. Clearly, the rock media had no choice but to sit up and take notice. If this was the album that put NIN on the road to success, the release in 1992 of the *Broken* mini-album stamped hard on the accelerator. Much more guitar-based, it was a sonic attack of self-hate and rabid energy, Reznor psychoanalysing himself in vivid detail. Songs like 'Wish' and 'Happiness In Slavery' remain about as dynamic and affecting as music in the nineties gets. More videos emerged, some too unpleasant to be shown uncut.

Reznor, now a major star, was on a roll, but his feelings of alienation and self-hatred only seemed to deepen. He recorded his third album, 1994's *The Downward Spiral*, in the house where Charles

NAILS

Manson's followers murdered actress Sharon Tate in 1969. Working in solitude in this horrific setting, Reznor opened up his inner self to even closer scrutiny, documenting in words and sound his worsening frustration and despair. The result was a quite astonishing album that encompassed everything from gentle piano-based songs to crescendos of tormented mayhem. 'Hurt' was a beautiful ballad on the subject of self-discovery, while 'Eraser' was a maelstrom of blank noise, with Reznor screaming in impotent rage just below the surface. In a youth culture that was shortly to be traumatised by Kurt Cobain's suicide, the album was understood by many, and sold in its millions.

Unlike Cobain, Reznor has always been able to deal with his personal demons through the power of his music, and through his performance. The band's 1994–5 world tour provided audiences with the biggest theatrical spectacle seen in rock since the days of Kiss. A NIN show is not just five blokes standing on a stage – it's a futuristic assault on all the senses. The band have worked hard on their image, painting their flesh white and dyeing their hair jet black to create stark, visual effects. They have turned a blind eye to grunge, bringing entertainment and glamour back to a defiantly colourless rock scene. Virtually the biggest live attraction in America, NIN sold out New York's legendary Madison Square Garden in the record time of fourteen minutes. They also took the revived Woodstock festival by storm, appearing on stage smeared head to toe in mud, and blowing away any nostalgic whiffs of flower power and free love.

Reznor has been unwilling or unable to stop working. He has produced film soundtracks and has formed his own record label, Nothing Records, for whom he has produced such bands as Prick and Marilyn Manson. The latter, in particular, have enjoyed considerable success and may well be among the biggest bands in rock by the turn of the century. In America, Reznor has become the uncomfortable subject of teen idolatry. Every day, he receives bundles of poetry and cries for help from confused or depressed young people who believe that he is the only one with whom they can identify. Reznor's anguished lyrics address his own problems, and he is consequently a reluctant role model.

'I don't even know who *I* am,' he has said. 'I know what I don't believe in, I know what I've rejected, but I don't know what I *do* believe in. I don't trust people very much.'

By chance or by design, the music of NIN accurately reflects the confusion faced by young people in the ever-uncertain nineties. It also mirrors the emphasis placed on computers and technology over manpower. All in all, it leaves us with a powerful and terrifying statement about modern life. The creative genius of Trent Reznor, however, leaves us gasping for more.

STONE TEMPLE PILOTS

It is unlikely that even the most experienced gambler would have put money on Stone Temple Pilots becoming one of the biggest acts in America. In 1988, when Scott Weiland and Robert DeLeo were sewing the seeds of the band, rock radio was dominated by leather-clad rockers writing lyrics about girls and cars. Weiland and DeLeo were a couple of short-haired punks living just south of Los Angeles. The polished, super-commercial sounds that were prevalent at the time meant nothing to them. Instead, they shared an interest in alternative styles of music and supported the local club scene.

Their paths crossed for the first time at a Black Flag gig in Long Beach. Not only did they discover a similar taste in music, but Scott was a decent singer who had fronted a couple of punk bands, while Robert was an aspiring bassist looking to form a band. Furthermore, he had a brother who played guitar. Their friendship cemented, they began to compose songs on DeLeo's eight-track, mainly for their own amusement. It was when they recruited drummer Eric Kretz from a local band, and convinced DeLeo's guitar-playing brother, Dean, to play on some new demos, that things started to get serious. Dean DeLeo, cynical about the West Coast scene, had been living in New Jersey. However, when Dean found that his own musical aspirations were shared by his brother's new friends, he decided to leave New Jersey for good.

Weiland sympathised with Dean's misgivings about Los Angeles, and as Mighty Joe Young became Stone Temple Pilots, they shifted their attention to San Diego. It was here that they gigged incessantly, gaining confidence and cohesion, as well as writing some truly exceptional songs. By 1992, Seattle stars like Nirvana and Pearl Jam had overturned popular concepts about what was commercial and what wasn't. Completely by accident, Stone Temple Pilots found that their style of music was suddenly considered to be every record company's dream ticket. The band showcased in LA and were soon snapped up by Atlantic Records.

The first album, *Core*, was produced by Brendan O'Brien to spectacular effect. So delighted were the band with the dynamic, rounded sound that O'Brien achieved on their already masterful material that they have opted to record with him ever since. *Core* was an incendiary debut, buzzing with emotion and angst. Its release in 1992 quickly established Stone Temple Pilots as a very powerful new force.

ott Weiland

Weiland's vocal tones varied from a comforting croon to a throat-shredding roar. The sonic aggression of Dean DeLeo's guitar work had to be heard to be believed on tracks like 'Sex Type Thing' and 'Crackerman', while the sensitivity and social realism of Weiland's lyrics attracted many to the band's cause. As musicians and writers they had proved themselves immensely talented, their music more deft and eloquent than most of Seattle's output, and yet no less accessible.

For all this, the media despised the band, describing them as Pearl Jam copyists and generally shouting 'sell-out'. This claim was disturbingly inaccurate. Although the band had much in common with grunge, their agenda was quite different, owing more to punk and early metal bands like Sabbath and Zeppelin. Stone Temple Pilots were simply a superb new rock band, playing a contemporary brand of music. Despite the fact that *Core* sold four million copies – more than Alice In Chains' *Dirt* and Rage Against the Machine's debut put together – the media crucified them.

Scott Weiland, in particular, found it hard to cope with the combined pressure of media hatred and overnight stardom. The band began to experience personal difficulties and, sadder still for Weiland, drugs became an issue. In 1993, however, MTV honoured the band with the Music Video Award for Best New Band, one of seven awards the group were to pick up that year.

Their second album, *Purple*, hit the critics where it hurt. The media had no choice but to acknowledge it for the masterpiece that it was. This was an amazingly diverse rock album full of poignancy, emotion and urgency. 'Vasoline' and 'Unglued' were riotous anthems, but 'Big Empty', 'Still Remains' and the Zeppelin-tinged 'Pretty Penny' were truly breathtaking, only growing in beauty with repeated plays. This was certainly not a grunge album. Unsurprisingly, it entered the U.S. album chart at Number One, where it remained for a further fortnight. In a few short years Stone Temple Pilots had gone from being a faceless garage band in San Diego to ranking as one of the biggest rock acts in the world. They had done it without the backing of the press. They had done it purely because lots of people loved their music.

l r Dean Deleo, Robert Deleo, Eric Kretz, Scott Weiland

By March 1996, when they released their third album, sales of *Core* and *Purple* totalled 11 million in the States alone. The latest offering, intriguingly titled *Tiny Music – Songs from the Vatican Gift Shop* sees the band continuing to diversify in all directions. Unfortunately, their main adversary is no longer the press, but Scott Weiland's spiralling dependency on drugs. During a blaze of news coverage, the singer was arrested for possession of hard drugs, and was placed under probation. Mortified by guilt, he arranged for Hole's Courtney Love to read a letter expressing his 'sorrow and embarrassment' on Californian radio station K-ROQ. In the letter, Weiland admitted that he was suffering from 'the disease of drug addiction' and had been 'a hypocrite to his social ideals'.

Unfortunately, Weiland then breached the conditions of his probation, missing an appointment with a drugs counsellor, and failed to turn up for band rehearsals. Instead, the troubled singer has been forcibly placed in a rehab unit, effectively ending the band's plans for 1996.

'It's really beautiful when we write a song and then give it to Scott,' said Dean DeLeo. 'What he adds is so satisfying that it brings it all to another level.' Weiland, undoubtedly, will be a hard man to replace, if indeed it is possible to replace him at all. The millions of fans who took Stone Temple Pilots at face value, and catapulted them to fame, will just have to pray that such a decision will never have to be made.

FEAR FACTORY

The biggest noise to have come out of LA in recent years belongs to lethal cyber-metallers Fear Factory. It is the sound of *Demanufacture*, their second full-length album and an aural mauling of the deadliest kind. *Demanufacture* is the sound of a band coming of age in the most spectacular, explosive manner. In grim detail, Fear Factory reflect the tense, polluted society from which they came. Their extreme metal leanings are tempered by computer-generated industrial effects and outrageous use of melody. You might expect proper, singable melodies to be impossible in such a context, but this is one band intent on smashing down all the usual boundaries.

All in all, Fear Factory are the embodiment of state-of-the-art nineties havoc.

Frontman Burton C. Bell, the band's charismatic visual and lyrical focus, was born in Texas, but moved with his mother and stepfather to North Virginia at the age of sixteen, where he graduated from high school. At age eighteen, Bell struck out on his own, eventually settling in Los Angeles in 1989. Like most cities, LA had its areas where it was simply not safe to go.

'When I moved there from Washington DC, it was a total culture shock,' recalls the frontman. 'You can sense the racism in the air. People grow up in their own little areas, not experiencing other types of people, unlike most other cities. That's where fear comes in, and from fear you get racial hatred and gang warfare.'

Bell had grown up listening to a variety of music, establishing a diverse taste that encompassed everything from country to punk. He had even been a fan of glam rockers Ratt until a friend at school introduced him to punk. In LA, Bell lived in a large, communal house with several others, including the other members of the hardcore band he was playing with. Also resident was guitarist Dino Cazares, who came to Bell's gigs and liked his style. Pretty soon, Burton was persuaded to join Dino's band, which already included drummer Raymond Herrera. Bassist Christian Olde Wolbers was introduced to the band by Biohazard, whilst he was visiting LA from Belgium. Wolbers was so impressed that he never went home.

After eighteen months spent honing their craft, Fear Factory were signed by Roadrunner Records. Their debut album, *Soul of a New Machine*, was released in 1992, and an EP, *Fear is the Mindkiller*, followed in 1993. It wasn't until 1995, however, and the release of *Demanufacture*, that Fear Factory were thrust into the spotlight. Their combination of computers and melody enhanced their already murderously heavy output and won them many new friends.

'It was something we were always striving for,' says Burton. 'At first it was all pretty primitive because we couldn't afford the computers we needed. Raymond had a machine rigged up to his drum kit that could trigger various sounds, but at least we were making an effort to be different. Once we were signed and on a budget, we were able to delve deeper and deeper into the technical side. Dino started producing all these techno effects and playing our songs over them. We were amazed at how well it all came together.'

While the first album acted as an introduction to Fear Factory,

All in all, Fear Factory are the embodiment of state-of-the-art nineties havoc.

'All the lyrics are based on personal feelings or experiences of the band,' confesses Burton

Fear Factory l r Dino Cazares, Burton C.Bell, Christian Olde Wolbers, Raymond Herrera

Demanufacture was their most complete statement. It proved to be an album of frightening intensity that properly realised the band's vision. Throughout the production, the band were assisted by Front Line Assembly's Rhys Fulber, who taught them much about the bionics of machines in music. The album was not just musically devastating, but lyrically inspiring, conjuring up many enduring, sometimes nightmarish images. Many of their songs, such as 'Self Bias Resistor', 'Replica' and 'Zero Signal' involve a central character who has suffered a variety of mental and physical abuses, and yet has had the courage to overcome.

'All the lyrics are based on personal feelings or experiences of the band,' confesses Burton. 'I've taken those feelings and compiled them together to create multi-faceted pictures and, hopefully, pretty strong statements. I consider myself a fairly left wing, poetic kind of person, and I like to write lyrics in story form. Some of the songs can be therapeutic. Others are like wrestling with personal demons...'

Fear Factory's endless roadwork and snowballing fan base caused their profile to grow dramatically in a very short space of time. Their European tour, which was presented in association with MTV's *Headbangers' Ball*, proved so popular that several gigs had to be switched to larger venues than originally planned. An appearance at Castle Donington's Monsters of Rock Festival in 1996 was further confirmation of Fear Factory's arrival on the world stage. Even million-selling chart-toppers the Prodigy took an interest, and offered to remix various tracks from *Demanufacture*.

The fruits of the Prodigy's coalition with the band can be heard on *Remanufacture*, an album of razor-sharp remixes. Another studio album from Fear Factory will undoubtedly put them up amongst metal's elite. They have the potential to be as big as any metal act in the world, and have already displayed the tenacity that will keep them there. The Fear Factory experience was fittingly summed up by *Kerrang!* magazine in November, 1995: 'Never in the field of human conflict has there been a band quite like Fear Factory...Walls trembled. Rib cages shook. Limbs were twisted. Vision became blurred. It *hurt*."

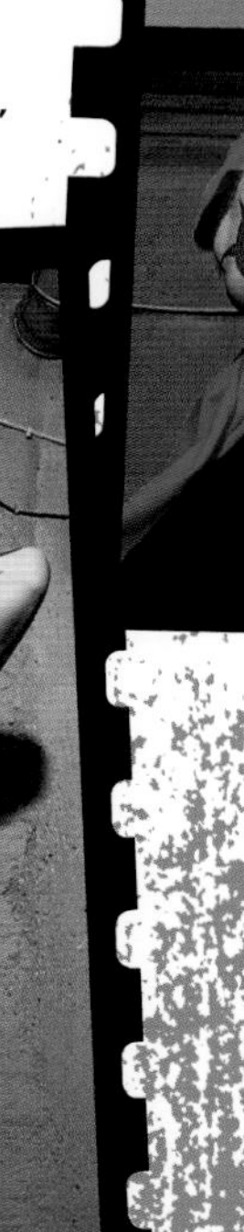

Burton C.Bell

Don't listen to Korn's album on your own – you never know quite what demons it will summon forth.

KORN

There are few bands liable to generate as much fear and loathing as Korn. The American quintet have taken tips from the likes of Biohazard and Prong. Low-slung, filthy riffs and insistent rhythms form the nucleus for Korn's contorted songs of menace and sickness. But just how sick are Korn? Judging by the lyrics and artwork of their eponymously titled debut album, it would appear that the Sony-signed Korn are sicker than a slew of video nasties.

Thankfully, Korn are also deeply gifted. They have managed to hit on a style that is like no other. The heaviness belongs to Pantera, the distortion to Prong, and the insanity generated by Jonathan Davis' ragged vocal tones is almost redolent of Nine Inch Nails. On top of all that, the band are masters of suspenseful songwriting, building their torrid anthems gradually, allowing audience tension to rise, before descending upon them in solid brick walls of sound. They toy around with unusual noises and effects in their quieter moments, endeavouring to maintain their sinister aura. Everything is deviously laid out so that you're never sure what's lurking just around the corner. Don't listen to Korn's album on your own – you never know quite what demons it will summon forth.

The group were formed in Bakersfield, California during 1989, though it has taken several years for their black magic to reach its full potential. It was not until 1993, and the recruitment of Davis, that the band finally began to gel. Davis, who had initially been influenced by Duran Duran and had fronted a band called Sex Art, was already acquiring a reputation for his bitter, throaty vocal style. He also brought with him the incredible idea of using bagpipes within a rock band, a trait that has stayed with the group to this day. The monster named Korn was now ready to wreak chaos out of all that stood before it.

The band were signed to Immortal Records, a division of Sony Music. Their debut album was recorded at Indigo Ranch Studios in Malibu with up and coming producer Ross Robinson who went on to produce albums for Sepultura, Deftones and Manhole. While the album was no overnight sensation, Korn quickly acquired an enviable cult status. Similarly happening rock luminaries, notably Machine Head frontman Robb Flynn, fell in love with the band's relentless, unforgiving style, and tipped them for greatness.

Jonathan Davis

'I love Korn,' announced Robb, 'they're one of my favourite bands... just awesome. I was attracted to them because they have a unique sound. The singer has a good voice. He conveys a lot of emotion and conviction, and they have some heavy-ass riffs.'

MTV quickly saw the potential in Korn, and began to play their video for 'Blind'. It was a massive success, and the album went on to sell over 500,000 copies in the States alone. The videos for 'Clown' and 'Shoots and Ladders' were also championed by *Headbangers' Ball* in Europe.

In an exclusive *Headbangers' Ball* interview in early 1996, when Korn were supporting Ozzy Osbourne across stadiums in America, Jonathan told Vanessa Warwick about the album.

'It's about being an outcast,' he revealed. 'It was

my outlet to get out everything that made me mad as a kid. I went through a lot as a kid and it was great to finally get a lot of things off my chest.'

Korn can boast a truly tasteless album cover featuring a small girl on a swing overshadowed by an ominous, Freddy Krueger type figure, but they don't stop there. The album's final track, 'Daddy', is a horrific look at child abuse, a song so unsettling that the band refuse to talk about it or play it live.

Korn's follow-up album, *Life is Peachy*, released in late '96, entered the US *Billboard* charts at number 3 and looks certain to catapult the band to international stardom. After a sold-out European tour in early '97 Korn returned to the US to play on the Lollapalozza festival. So life is looking very peachy indeed for the five young men from Bakersville who are shaping up to be one of the most important and influential metal bands of the late nineties.

Drummer David

'It's about being an outcast,' he revealed. 'It was my outlet to get out everything that made me mad as a kid. I went through a lot as a kid and it was great to finally get a lot of things off my chest.'

Guitarist Fieldy

l r Adam Duce, Robb Flynn, Cave McClain, Logan Mader
Far right Robb Flynn

It was inevitable that a band like Machine Head would eventually come churning out of the gun-crazed, drug-infested streets of Oakland, California. Put together in 1992 by former Vio-lence and Forbidden member Robb Flynn, Machine Head have made musical brutality into their own sick art form. Their high-volume assault offers both aural and lyrical descriptions of life in one of the most violent cities in America. The band are as hard as they come, a heavy metal answer to the confrontational realism of rap.

It's all too easy for fans to look at Machine Head's meteoric rise, and wrongly assume that the band have never had to fight for attention, and have simply never paid their dues. Little could be further from the truth. Flynn, Machine Head's imposing singer and guitarist, has spent most of his life on the Bay Area thrash scene, firstly going to watch the likes of Exodus and the young Metallica rip it up in small, seedy clubs, and then taking an active part in the scene himself. Originally a member of ferocious thrash metallers Forbidden, Flynn then played guitar with Vio-lence, with whom he recorded three albums, and experienced a certain degree of notoriety.

An adopted child, born in 1968, Flynn discovered heavy metal in his early teens, at about the same time that he discovered drugs. The spell cast upon him by Black Sabbath was so powerful that he even began to take the lyrics seriously, pretending to be a satanist, and shrieking devilish nonsense to people at school. Living in a tough society, where gang warfare and drive-by shootings appeared in the news as regularly as the weather forecast, Flynn found his release in the energy and the outrage of bands like Possessed and Exodus. Bands just didn't come any heavier. It was only his infatuation with the ultra-violence of thrash that steered him away from a life of crime.

After five years with Vio-lence, the band dissolved. Flynn had almost killed himself with heroin, and the group had nowhere else to go. Meanwhile, Machine Head's future lead guitarist Logan Mader and bassist Adam Duce had been school friends, united by their interest in music and hard drugs. Drummer Chris Kontos, too, was a recovering drug addict. It seemed impossible, in downtown Oakland, not to be sucked into the social whirlpool of selling and using heroin. If you weren't dealing in drugs, you were probably selling firearms. Or both. Flynn, Mader, Duce and Kontos, on meeting for the first time, at least opted for something more constructive.

Machine Head's first album, *Burn My Eyes*, was released by Roadrunner Records in 1994. It was a furious cry from the streets that successfully blended the power of Bay Area thrash with contemporary grooves. There were harsh melodies, the occasional industrial tendency, and, above all, total,

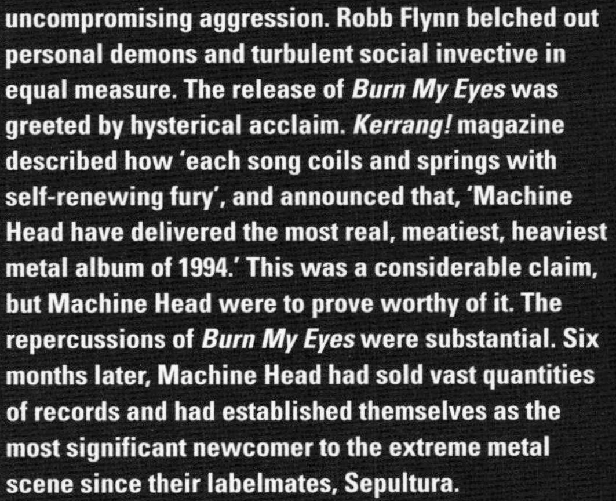

uncompromising aggression. Robb Flynn belched out personal demons and turbulent social invective in equal measure. The release of *Burn My Eyes* was greeted by hysterical acclaim. *Kerrang!* magazine described how 'each song coils and springs with self-renewing fury', and announced that, 'Machine Head have delivered the most real, meatiest, heaviest metal album of 1994.' This was a considerable claim, but Machine Head were to prove worthy of it. The repercussions of *Burn My Eyes* were substantial. Six months later, Machine Head had sold vast quantities of records and had established themselves as the most significant newcomer to the extreme metal scene since their labelmates, Sepultura.

Finally kicking their heroin habits, the band toured successfully with Slayer, but were very quickly in a position to headline themselves. Both MTV and *Kerrang!* continued to champion them, and in July 1995 the band were duly honoured by receiving two *Kerrang!* Awards, for Best New International Act, and for Best Promo Video, for 'Davidian'. The viewers of *Headbangers' Ball* voted for the latter category, and the award was presented by Vanessa Warwick. Machine Head's reputation continued to grow, and was cemented further by a sensational appearance at the Donington Monsters of Rock Festival. Supporting Metallica, the group produced a set of paralysing fury, showering the 70,000-strong audience with torrential energy.

Sadly, personal difficulties led to a parting of the ways with drummer Chris Kontos. By the time the band repaired to Oakland to record second album, *The More Things Change*, former Sacred Reich drummer Dave McClain had joined the fold. New tracks like 'Struck a Nerve' and the slower, moodier 'Ten Ton Hammer' saw the band becoming ever more intense in attitude, and ever more ugly in sound. With their new album, Machine Head have developed into an unstoppable force. Resistance has become futile.

WHITE ZOMBIE

Remember that scene in *Evil Dead II* when the hero is ambushed by a chainsaw-wielding ghoul in the shed? Whilst it's a gruesome scene full of chaos and bloodshed, it's also remarkably comical. Much the same can be said of the White Zombie experience. Larger then life, louder than hell and dressed up like the undead at a circus, White Zombie are the musical equivalent of a filthy, gas-guzzling juggernaut with some serious muscle in the engine department. Trashy sci-fi villains lost on planet earth, this band are nothing if not entertaining. Which is what music is supposed to be all about.

A group like this does not simply appear overnight. Frontman Rob Zombie's entire life has been one long rehearsal for this most sleazy and madcap of bands. Growing up in Massachusetts, the budding Zombie could find nothing to do apart from watch horror movies and play video games. School was mind-numbing, and he thought his home state a boring, dead-end place. Even the opening of a new McDonalds was a major event for Rob. All he wanted to do was make movies, or join a band, or draw comics. All he had for company was the TV.

l r Johnny Tempesta, Rob Zombie, Sean Yseult and J

Larger then life,
louder than hell and
dressed up like the
undead at a circus...

The evil dead Rob Zombie and friend

'I must have started watching TV at such an early age,' Rob told *Kerrang!* in 1995. 'My mom and dad never really cared what I watched. They didn't see it as particularly harmful. I'm still not sure whether it was or not.'

At the age of eighteen, Rob took his talent for outlandish art to college in New York. Unfortunately, his minuscule attention span was no better catered for here, but at least there were gigs to attend, and places to hang out. Rob enjoyed the over-the-top theatrics of bands like Kiss, but also had an interest in the darker, more macabre sounds of Black Sabbath. He met like-minded bassist Sean (pronounced Shauna) Yseult at a hardcore matinee, and decided to form a band which would fuse these influences together.

Neither of them were expecting too much from the band. It was just another outlet, an excuse to tour and enjoy life. In fact, White Zombie toured relentlessly, engaging an ever-shifting line-up, until settling on guitarist J and drummer Johnny Tempesta. Tongue-in-cheek attempts were made to emulate Kiss, the band setting off stink bombs on stage to create smoke, and stealing bright lights from construction sites to be positioned behind the drum kit. Such audacious antics and a string of independently released singles caught the attention of Caroline Records. On a minimal budget, White Zombie recorded two albums, *Soul Crusher* and *Make Them Die Slowly*.

Both releases failed to set the world alight, but by now the major label Geffen were on their case. In 1992, White Zombie released *La Sexorcisto: Devil Music Volume One*, a messily produced B-movie in sound.

However, with the band touring endlessly and filming promo videos, they gained the patronage of MTV's *Beavis and Butt-Head* and were quickly embraced by America's youth. They even scored a minor hit single with road anthem 'Thunderkiss '65'. Their low-budget album was achieving the impossible.

Their follow up, 1995's unfeasibly titled *Astro Creep: 2000 Songs of Love, Destruction and Other Synthetic Delusions of the Electric Head* was the album that broke White Zombie worldwide. This time they benefited from an enormous production, courtesy of Terry Date (Pantera, Soundgarden). Industrial elements, crushing riffs and an array of weird samples allowed the likes of 'Super-Charger Heaven' and 'I, Zombie' to leap out of the speakers in 3-D and gobble up listeners all over the world. 'We wanted to take the raw, live thing we do and add to it this super-techno stuff,' explained Rob.

Sean Yseult

White Zombie were now able to stage the sort of vast, psychotic freakshows they had always dreamed of. Synchronised explosions, crucified dummies and a real sense of event were now filling amphitheatres not only in America, but in all four corners of the globe. White Zombie are truly a nineties phenomenon. This goofy, eccentric band have ignored all prevailing trends in music, and exist in their own unique genre. They have been gleefully hailed by a generation of metal fans starved of genuine, larger-than-life rock stars.

White Zombie

Just prior to publication, White Zombie announced that they would be taking an indefinite break to allow Rob to work on tv and film projects. Fans can only hope this is not the end of the road for this rollercoaster of a band.

TYPE O NEGATIVE

If you're in search of a different kind of power, Type O Negative are the strangest of the strange.

If you're in search of a different kind of power, Type O Negative are the strangest of the strange. Essentially, they are the dark and dangerous offspring of frontman Peter Steele, a towering giant with granite-like features and jet black hair. Throughout his career, Steele has welcomed controversy with open arms, becoming a master of self-publicity in the process. After inauspicious beginnings, he has developed Type O Negative into one of America's most compelling new rock bands.

Peter Steele was born 'somewhere in Northern Europe' in 1962. Like Rob Zombie, he quickly acquired an abiding passion for horror films and monsters. Steele considered himself fortunate to have five impressionable sisters, an obvious target for his trickery and practical jokes. Living in America in the eighties, his sisters could finally relax as he transferred his attentions to hardcore, playing in bands like Fallout and, more significantly, Carnivore.

Peter Steele

It was during this time that Steele acquired a reputation as a sexist and racist, with songs like 'Male Supremacy' cited as particularly offensive. In fact, Steele's only concern was to manipulate the media into portraying him as some kind of American anti-hero, thereby guaranteeing stacks of publicity. It was a ploy he developed further with his next project, Type O Negative. Steele assembled the band in Brooklyn during 1990, and set about causing as much indignation as possible.

The first album, 1991's *Slow, Deep and Hard*, and 1992's live EP *Origin of the Faeces* were deliberately engineered to cause offence. Few could plumb their way beneath Steele's stony-faced exterior to find the true irony beneath. The frontman's massive build and dry sense of humour simply scared most people away.

'It's amusing how people panic when confronted with something outside the norm,' he told the press. 'I like to make heads spin, and I do it really well.'

The third album, *Bloody Kisses*, did just that. Eschewing the easy option of recording another hardcore album, Steele produced a magnificent rock opus, replete with a gothic veneer and a subtle sense of melody. Lyrically, it dealt dangerously with sex and religion, upsetting many, but enthralling far more. With the likes of 'Christian Woman' and 'Blood and Fire', Steele spun out simple songs into long, graceful epics. The religious overtones and classical allusions only deepened the album's mystery. It was a bold and polished product from a band better known for sheer bludgeon.

After a slow start, the album, released by Roadrunner, began to sell in massive quantities, and a tour with Nine Inch Nails and Pantera followed. All of a sudden, America could not get enough of this intoxicating, curious new band. In 1995 the once-reviled Steele was offered $2,000 to pose nude for the U.S. edition of *Playgirl* magazine. He complied, and spent the money on new equipment for the band.

On 2 September 1996, the group followed up *Bloody Kisses* with a new album, *October Rust*. This gloriously dark and decadent record had all the makings of a natural successor to *Bloody Kisses*. This time, the musical goal was 'sonic saturation – as much sonic information as possible. Each time you listen to the album you're going to hear something else,' promised Steele.

Type O Negative have finally reaped the rewards of their frontman's carefully engineered publicity campaign. With the band's ever-enlarging fan base baying for more, *October Rust* is proving to be a spinner of more than just heads!

No frills,

no fancy guitar work,

no classically trained singer,

just four guys blasting out their

frustrations with intelligence,

sincerity and charisma.

There has always been a certain thrill at the idea of four guys simply plugging in and exploding all over the stage. In New York, a hardcore punk scene has existed almost from the days when three-chord savagery first reared its ugly head. No frills, no fancy guitar work, no classically trained singer, just four guys blasting out their frustrations with intelligence, sincerity and charisma. In the mid-nineties, pop has crossed over with punk, creating platinum-selling acts like Green Day and Offspring. This renewed interest in the re-emerging ideology of punk has led many to seek out the true exponents of the art. The thriving New York scene is at last to have its day.

Civ got together almost as a joke. No one seriously expected the band to take off, let alone land a major record deal. Sammy, Arthur, Charlie and Civ himself were simply four buddies who had played in bands before and had always supported the local scene. The idea behind the band Civ was just to record a few seven-inch singles for independent release. However, their first jam session revealed an incredible intensity and a definite fusion of ideas. Everyone involved in the band could suddenly see the potential.

In the mid-eighties, 'straight edge' began to emerge as a dominant force on the New York scene. Contrary to their reputation, hardcore bands would strive for sobriety and abstinence, writing strong, political lyrics which encouraged young fans to take a more responsible attitude to their own lives and the world around them. Under the influence of Ray Cappo, who eventually went on to form Shelter, hardcore was becoming a happier, more positive scene.

Cappo toured America with Youth of Today, a band that also featured future Civ drummer Sammy, then just fourteen years old. Cappo became an expressive spokesman for the movement that was to dominate the scene for several years. He also founded Revelation Records, which provided an opportunity for the scene's bands to make their own records. Revelation released debut albums by such influential New York bands as Quicksand, Sick of it All and Gorilla Biscuits.

Civ, Arthur and Sammy were all members of the latter, a band that caused a considerable stir until its demise in 1992. Another ex-Gorilla Biscuits member, Quicksand's Walter Schreifels, was asked to produce Civ's debut album, after the band had secured a highly desirable deal with Lava/Atlantic Records. The album, *Set Your Goals*, was released in 1995, having been co-produced by the legendary Don Fury, well known in New York circles for his work with Helmet, Quicksand and Warrior Soul. Civ's policy had always been to work with people who had been personal friends on the scene, and they saw no reason to stop now just because they had a big record deal in the bag.

Deservedly, *Set Your Goals* was a major hit. It brought Civ's live energy into sharp focus, comprising no less than seventeen tough, direct songs with catchy melodies. Influenced by everyone from the Sex Pistols to Adam and the Ants, this was an album that combined positive messages with rushes of adrenalin. The band even acknowledged the influence of fellow New Yorkers Kraut, with a cover of 'All Twisted'.

Civ were certainly not the only band to emerge from the scene. Their friends Sick of it All, whose frontman Lou Koller guested on Civ's hit 'Can't Wait One Minute More', signed to EastWest America, and won many followers with their heavier, more aggressive style. Pro-Pain found similar favour, and Shelter, Ray Cappo's new band, were signed by Roadrunner. Now a born-again follower of the Krishna movement, Cappo continues to preach positive, articulate messages in both music and writing. He is the author of a book entitled *In Defense of Reality*, and with Shelter he has spread the word on tours with Green Day, Type O Negative and old colleagues Sick of it All.

Bands like Civ and Shelter are products of a generation that is thinking for itself and coming to its own conclusions. In songs like 'Choices Made' and 'Do Something', Civ urge their followers to stand up for their beliefs while resisting fads and trends. 'Solid Bond' is a celebration of friendship. The words 'hardcore' and 'positive' used in the same sentence may seem a contradiction in terms to outsiders, but the New York scene is proving that today's youth are not the useless generation that many would have you believe. The kids, as someone once said, are all right.

THE WILDHEARTS

Few were truly prepared for the impact of the nailbomb known as the Wildhearts. Here was a band not only with talent and musical integrity, but with a burning desire to turn convention on its head, making music that was both accessible and utterly individual. Giving off the same tension and sense of danger as the Sex Pistols before them, the Wildhearts are a law unto themselves.

Their story, fuelled by rumour and hearsay, is full of controversy, all of which has been well documented elsewhere. In a sense, it has been unfortunate that such friction has been allowed to detract from the music, which from the Wildhearts has never been anything less than spectacular.

The band's mainstay is the enigmatic Ginger, a supremely talented and imaginative creative force whose one-to-one relationship with his fans has quite rightly always been more important to him than kowtowing to the media. Ginger was briefly a member of the Quireboys, recording two singles with them, before leaving to mastermind his own operation.

The first Wildhearts release was a scorching four-track EP, titled *Mondo Akimbo A-Go-Go*, launched in 1992 to rapturous acclaim. No blueprint really exists for the Wildhearts' nonconformist sense of style and renegade attitude, but the band's capabilities were brought home to one and all in resounding fashion. Hard-living bass player Danny McCormack (whose brother Chris is now a leading light in British hotshots 3 Colours Red) began to epitomise the Wildhearts' attitude, while guitarist CJ (now with Honeycrack) and drummer Bam were the perfect foils to Ginger's troubled brilliance. Early live shows were the stuff of legend, and the band's profile increased with the release of a second EP, *Don't Be Happy...Just Worry.*

Bam was purely on loan from Dogs D'Amour, and by the time the band came to record their classic 1993 debut album, *Earth Vs the Wildhearts*, he had been replaced by Stid, who was himself to leave the band afterwards to be replaced by former Radio Moscow drummer Ritch. In Britain, the two EPs had brought anticipation of the full length album to fever pitch, and no one was disappointed by what was delivered. The band's ability to layer gorgeous harmonies onto riffs of phenomenal heaviness was perhaps their greatest single strength. They had both a pop and metal mentality, and combined them to magnificent effect. 'Greetings From Shitsville', 'TV Tan' and the energised quasi-Thrash of 'Suckerpunch' were

GIVING OFF THE SAME TENSION AND SENSE OF DANGER AS THE SEX PISTOLS BEFORE THEM, THE WILDHEARTS ARE A LAW UNTO THEMSELVES.

dizzying aural rampages, and set rock clubs afire all over their homeland. Lengthier tracks, like 'Everlone', demonstrated the breadth of the band's repertoire.

The band's work rate was second to none. They unleashed a previously unavailable single in the form of 'Caffeine Bomb', a headlong stampede of a song, which boasted a controversial video featuring CJ and Ginger throwing up into each others faces. The offending matter was actually just vegetable soup, and besides, nothing could stop the song from storming into the British Top Twenty. Similar success was achieved with the next single, a double A-side featuring an off-the-wall folk lilt called 'Geordie In Wonderland'.

A compilation of out-takes and bonus tracks entitled *Fishing For Luckies* saw general release, although apparently not with the band's approval, and it wasn't until their second album proper, in 1995, that fans were given a glimpse of how rapidly the band were developing. Boasting the tongue-in-cheek title of *P.H.U.Q*, the album contained a diversity of material and a consistency of quality that made it at least the equal of their debut. The video for 'I Wanna Go Where the People Go', a gushing pop rocker with an enormous hook, was a favourite on MTV, and the band followed it up with the equally infectious 'Just in Lust'.

To do their new material justice, the Wildhearts recruited keyboard player Willie Dowling for live work, but it was with Dowling that CJ was to depart to form Honeycrack. A period of soul searching and record company friction followed. The band engaged various personnel on guitar, and even toyed with the idea of playing as a trio with Ginger handling all guitar parts. Finally, the previously unknown Jef Streatfield proved the perfect addition to the ranks, and a series of sensational UK tours followed.

Dissatisfaction with record company EastWest almost led to a permanent split, but thankfully the band have persevered, partly due to the frenzied support of their fans. A 1996 European tour with Antipodean metal titans AC/DC may not have been the ideal platform for this explosive young band, but it at least gave them the chance to display their wares to new territories and new audiences. Unpredictable to the end, the Wildhearts stand tall among the most influential British bands of the decade.

WOMEN IN ROCK

VANESSA WARWICK

'I'm a very strong believer in having a positive mental attitude, and believing in yourself. Despite what people say, there are lots of opportunities, and having the right attitude is vital not only to your work, but to life in general.'

Vanessa Warwick is talking about some of the qualities that have helped pave her way to success and influence at MTV. Since 1991, Vanessa has been the full-time producer and presenter of MTV's specialist rock/metal show, *Headbangers' Ball*. In those years, Vanessa has gained a reputation not only for her well-informed and pertinent interview angles, but for her constant assessment of the show's format, keeping in synch with the times and with audience demand. Her lifestyle, which involves working with most of the top names in rock as well as continual travel, is the envy of many a viewer.

Vanessa is quick to acknowledge how fortunate she feels to have found such a niche. 'I can honestly say that I love every minute of my job. To me, there isn't a negative side to it. People often think that I don't know how lucky I am, but believe me, I do. I count my blessings every single day. I suppose the only vaguely bad thing is that I do get exceedingly over-tired, usually when I've got to work after an eleven-hour flight.'

Few people arrive in such a job without possessing special talents or ceaseless dedication, and Vanessa is no exception. There are few roles in the music business that she has not sampled at first hand. She has played in bands, managed bands, worked as a PA, has written for *Metal Hammer* and *Metal Forces*, and has worked for several record companies operating freelance promotions, press and marketing. By gradually making a name for herself through her varied work and increasing list of contacts, her talents were soon picked up by MTV.

'When I heard about MTV starting up, I thought, "Music? Television? Sounds good to me!" and I was literally offered one day's work filing,' she recalls. 'As soon as I came here, I really believed that this was where my future lay. They needed a PA for a few weeks, so I did that, and three months later, having never left, I was offered a full-time job working as a production assistant on MTV's very first metal show, *MTV's Metal Hammer. Headbangers' Ball* started in 1990, and a year on from that, I asked if I could be a reporter. My first job was covering an Overkill gig. Unfortunately, there was a riot outside, and on my first-ever piece to camera you can see fire bombs flying around behind me. Thankfully, things got better after that.'

The daughter of an airline pilot, Vanessa spent her childhood in many different parts of the world, and quickly became accustomed to a nomadic existence. Obliged to attend a strict private girls' school, she soon found a release in music. She was attracted by the energy and excitement of bands like Iron Maiden and AC/DC. Restless, and craving a diversion from school's bland imperative, she did

'When I heard about MTV starting up, I thought, "Music? Television? Sounds good to me!"'

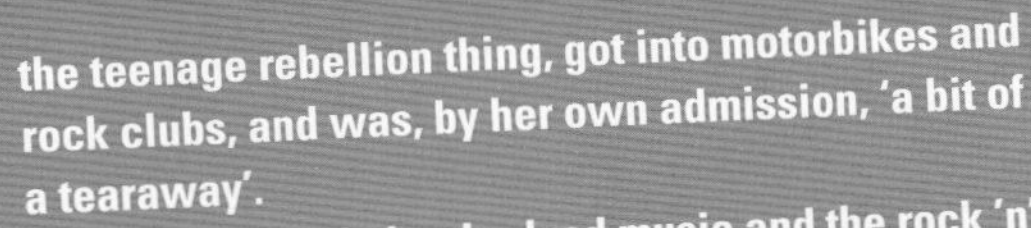

the teenage rebellion thing, got into motorbikes and rock clubs, and was, by her own admission, 'a bit of a tearaway'.

Her interest in hard-edged music and the rock 'n' roll lifestyle had been ignited, never to be extinguished. Now, although considerably more responsible (she is accountable for every facet of the programme, including the budget), her enthusiasm remains undiminished. Producing *Headbangers' Ball* has not come as a result of a media course, but of experience gained through working for bands and companies on her own initiative.

'I have to be as organised as possible,' she says, subconsciously nodding towards her surprisingly tidy desk, 'because as the show's producer, the buck stops with me, and I have to take responsibility. A typical week involves checking out all the new releases and videos, formatting the running order of the show, writing scripts, and editing separate features to be slotted into the show. On top of that, I'm also working on projects not related to production, like booking flights, hotels and camera crews if I'm filming abroad. I'm also writing proposals to record companies regarding their artists, and sorting out the budget. I do also read every letter that comes to the show, and I do try to reply to as many as possible.

'We're under constant pressure not only to keep up with the times, but to produce a show that gets good ratings, so audience feedback is vital. I think of *Headbangers' Ball* as representing the cutting edge of music. We're the first in with new talent, but also provide a good mix of music, covering all genres of rock.'

Vanessa came into the world of rock at a time when much of heavy metal was horrendously sexist, and strong female role models were a rarity. Her first female hero was Debbie Harry ('She inspired me to reach for the bleach!'), and she still harbours ambitions to interview Madonna. In the nineties, women have progressed in many different areas, bringing with them fresh ideas and perspectives. For all the strong-minded women that have been successful in their particular field, gender remains an unavoidable issue. Even now, Vanessa is constantly called upon to debunk various myths surrounding the image of the female presenter.

'I certainly perceive myself as a presenter, and not a VJ,' she stresses. 'VJs are often ex-models who say, "Look at me, I'm attractive, I'm fashionable, and I'm saying something that may perhaps be of interest to you." That's not where I'm coming from. I believe that the bands should be the stars of the show, and they don't need some silly bimbo flirting with them and trying to steal their limelight. If people like the way I look, then fine, but I always approach my work from a journalistic point of view.

'My job is to encourage bands to open up and express themselves. Eddie Vedder gave me a world-exclusive interview just four days after the death of Kurt Cobain, and both Eddie and I were actually crying by the end of it. He later thanked me for asking sympathetic questions and not putting him in a difficult situation. I'd be very insulted if someone regarded me as a bimbo, as I regard myself as being quite intelligent and well informed. I'd like to think that I'm perceived as a strong woman who has succeeded in a male-dominated environment on my own merits.'

Having worked her way up the ladder within such an environment, Vanessa is in an ideal position to comment on the advances made by women in rock during the last decade. Being part of that advance herself, she now regards the eighties as being a bad time for those female musicians hoping to be perceived as serious artists.

'Women were seen either as groupies, hangers on, or as people to look sexy in videos. A lot of bands, like Vixen, played on their looks too much and actually didn't need to, because they were really very good musicians. Eventually, they were a casualty of that. Grunge killed them off. Now women are coming forward in rock with their own look, personality and musical style, and are achieving credibility via that route. Believe in yourself, make contacts and learn from others. There are some very positive role models around now who make it easier for other women in rock to be taken seriously.'

To see one of them, you have only to set your video for MTV's *Headbangers' Ball*.

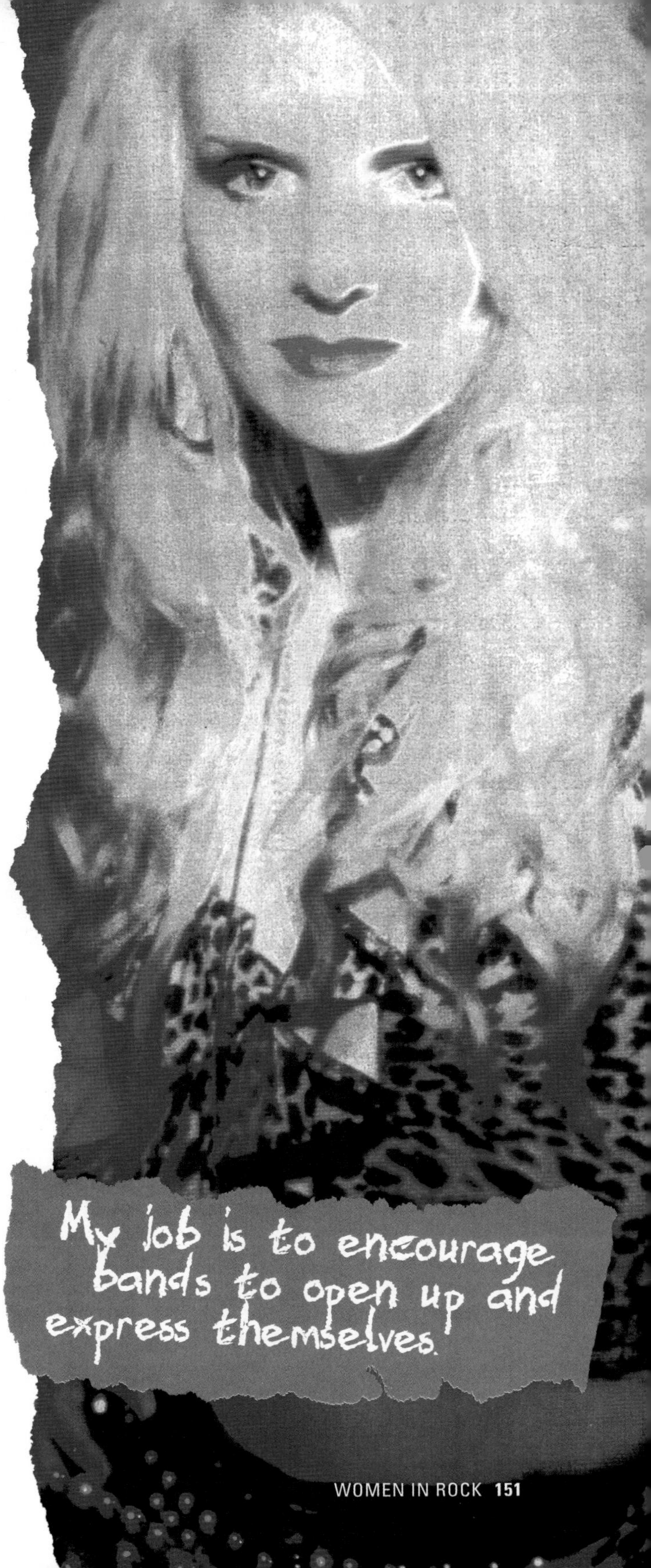

SHIRLEY MANSON

Shirley Manson

Garbage are among the brightest stars of a new wave of nineties rock acts. Although the band was initially seen as a vehicle for Nirvana producer Butch Vig's talents (Vig is Garbage's drummer as well as producer), their alluring singer Shirley Manson not only provides the group with a visual focus, but cloaks their sound in her own powerfully dark aura. With Shirley at the helm, Garbage have developed an enviable crossover potential, which has seen them win acclaim in rock, indie and pop circles. In Britain, they have enjoyed a succession of hit singles, including the Top Five smash 'Stupid Girl', all taken from their exotic debut album.

Unusually for a band who are closely tied with Seattle's grunge fraternity, their vocalist originates from Edinburgh in Scotland. A charismatic, slightly built singer, Shirley Manson combines grace and intelligence with an almost effortless stage presence. As such, she is one of rock's more bewitching figures.

Shirley's path to fame began with a small theatre company, and an interest in acting.

'Rather then taking an interest in music, music took an interest in me,' she muses. 'At theatre group I met a boy who had a band, and he invited me to join in an attempt to get me into bed. To be honest, it worked. I'm guilty as charged, m'lud.'

An appearance on MTV caught Butch Vig's eye, and the rest is history. As a teenager, Shirley had been influenced by punk, but it was the Pretenders' Chrissie Hynde who provided her with a role model.

'When I first saw her, I thought it was a dream come true,' she recalls. 'She stood there with her guitar hanging down by her hips, looking like the coolest person alive. When you're an adolescent girl, feeling vulnerable and inarticulate, connecting with a figure like her leads to a tremendous feeling of empowerment.'

However, being a woman in a rock group has never been the smoothest of rides. Although Shirley considers herself fortunate to be in an otherwise all-male but completely non-sexist group, she has no doubt that prejudice still exists in the business, lurking just beneath the surface.

'I've generally had very positive experiences with men in both my personal life and my career. My father is a wonderful man who has helped me to choose well. However, I read a quote in a book recently which said that women who want to get ahead have to bitch, nag and weep, and have to do all three for a long, long time. That can certainly be true. In the music business, women have to stand up and shout to be noticed. They have to be prepared to shout a lot louder than a male would.'

Whether or not the situation has improved in the last decade is a moot point. The likes of Vixen and Phantom Blue in the eighties were certainly talented, but were they ever really in control of their careers?

SHIRLEY MANSON (GARBAGE)

(GARBAGE)

Garbage Shirley Manson second left Butch Vig second right

Garbage are among the brightest stars of a new wave of nineties rock acts.

There is some music that is just uniquely female.

could want,' Shirley believes. 'If I was that famous myself, it would certainly be a responsibility, but I can think of worse role models. I've always been encouraged by strong women, and I've become strong myself. That alone is a good thing for a young girl to see in a woman.'

'I'd hesitate to say that it's improved,' says Shirley. 'In some areas it has, because there are more female artists selling records, but there are still some unbelievably old-fashioned attitudes present. That's part of life in general, not just the music business. Record company executives have had to sit up and take notice because there are immensely popular female artists like Alanis Morissette, who have started a renaissance for female singers and musicians.

'Females can often communicate things that standard male rock acts don't. The public are very interested in that, and it fascinates men just as much as it fascinates women. There are lots of male artists that I admire and have been moved by, but I think that women are generally better able to express themselves, particularly in identifying their own vulnerability. There is some music that is just uniquely female.'

For almost the first time, young female rock fans can look to the stage and see positive, acceptable female role models. Shirley Manson is one of them, a realistic and independent woman who uses her music to express both strength and weakness. She cites Hole's Courtney Love as being among the most influential women in rock.

'If Courtney can survive these dark times in her life, she will be the best role model a girl

Manhole. l-r. Scott Ueda, Rico Villasenor Tairrie B Marcelo Palomino

TAIRRIE B (MANHOLE)

Straight from the city of angels, Manhole's Tairrie B has exploded onto the scene with all the potency of a bullet from a gun. A European tour with Fear Factory has helped Tairrie to establish herself as one of the most forthright and outspoken women in rock. Manhole deliver a ferocious brand of hardcore rap metal, and Tairrie willingly seizes on subjects that have remained taboo for too long. Her belief in speaking her mind and her uncompromising approach to women's issues have probably earned her as many enemies as friends.

As a white girl rapper, initially signed as a solo artist to the specialist label run by Eazy E, founder of NWA, Ruthless Records, Tairrie found herself held back by sexism and racial hatred at every turn.

'It was a black, male-dominated world,' she recalls. 'Along comes this white girl who doesn't take any abuse, writes her own lyrics and isn't easily intimidated, and they suddenly got bitter. It was as if everyone was trying to gag me, and for a while, I felt threatened.'

Tairrie formed Manhole in an attempt to tackle the bigots and the bullies head on. Also featuring guitarist Scott Ueda, bassist Rico Villasenor and drummer Marcelo Palomino, the band's savage and traumatic debut, *All Is Not Well*, released by Noise Records in 1996, sees Tairrie addressing subjects such as street violence, sexism and the horrors of rape in profound, unflinching detail. Fuelled by anger, and with her terrific, blood-curdling vocals pushed to the fore, Tairrie stands up and screams where others have merely whispered. Hers is perhaps the strongest, most direct voice to have ever confronted women's issues in the rock/metal sphere.

'All the lyrics on the record are absolutely personal, except for the fact that I was never raped,' she says. 'Coming from a woman, a song about rape is much more real. No man will ever know how it feels to walk down a street at night, constantly in fear of rape. Women are scrutinised like commodities. That's why so many women have feelings of insecurity, getting boob jobs, losing weight, suffering physically and mentally. A twelve-year-old girl recently told me that she had been raped, and that she'd found strength in our music and my lyrics. That gave me chills. Everything seemed worthwhile and real.'

Tairrie is a gifted advocate of free speech. She has chosen to fight the way the establishment has treated women artists in rock. Although she believes that women have made great strides forward, she concedes that the industry is still controlled by men, many of whom have shaped female bands to their own specifications. All Tairrie is fighting for is an opportunity to speak the truth and be respected for it. She's here to put a message across, with her microphone and her talent, not her body.

'IF I NEED THERAPY I'LL GET UP ON STAGE AND SCREAM,' SHE SAYS.

'I'LL SHOUT. I'LL RAGE AND I'LL EVEN CRY SOMETIMES. MUSIC IS THERAPHY. AND MY THERAPHY IS MANHOLE.'

Personal exorcism Tairrie B on stage.

Courtney Love

COURTNEY LOVE

On both of her albums with Hole, but especially 1994's *Live Through This*, Courtney Love expresses her self, her *female* self, with guttural, heart-wrenching sincerity. It would be impossible for a male-fronted band to have written a song like 'Doll Parts', and even if they had, they could never have performed it with the same passion and honesty.

Courtney was born in 1965 in Oregon. Like her mother, she could never settle. When living in New Zealand, she was expelled from school and was returned to Oregon to attend reform school. At sixteen, however, she struck out on her own, wanting to travel as much as possible. She discovered she could earn money from stripping but, tiring of this degradation, moved to England to sample the mid-eighties punk scene in Liverpool.

Ever the wanderer, she soon returned to America, and briefly turned to acting. She continued to travel, singing with bands all over America, including a brief stint with Faith No More, and the Minneapolis-based act Sugar Baby Doll, which also featured Jennifer Finch and Kat Bjelland, soon to find their own success with L7 and Babes In Toyland. Back in LA, Courtney formed Hole.

The band, featuring drummer Patty Schemel, guitarist Eric Erlandson and bassist Kristin Pfaff, released their independent debut, *Pretty on the Inside*, in 1991. It was a disturbing album, with Courtney screaming and raving over discordant guitar noise. Songs like 'Teenage Whore' also provided her first taste of controversy. Courtney had been inspired by the all-female trio, Frightwig, a band of solid musicians. Above all else, she wanted to express herself in Hole, and that certainly didn't involve dressing up in skin-tight leather and acting like someone else's titillation device.

'The pool of women to play with is small,' she said. 'Girls' playing is passion and rage, and it can also be ugly and jarring. To deny my femininity and just rock out like a guy would not be part of evolution.'

In February 1992, Courtney married Nirvana frontman Kurt Cobain, and Hole signed a major deal with Geffen. Cynics looked on the union as being little more than a splendid career move, and, like so many suddenly burdened by celebrity status, Courtney suffered personality problems. The birth of a daughter, Frances Bean, on 18 August, and subsequent admissions to *Vanity Fair* that both she and Cobain had become heroin addicts before the pregnancy, caused outrage.

The release of *Live Through This* proved what Hole, and Courtney in particular, were capable of. Her uniquely tearful vocals formed the epicentre of twelve biting tracks varying from the restraint of 'Miss World' and 'Softer, Softest', to the raw, full-blooded attack of 'Plump' and 'She Walks On Me'. Though clearly influenced by Nirvana, this album gave Courtney a much needed outlet for her talents and frustrations. Several songs were to prove ominously prophetic.

Cobain's suicide in April 1994 has been well documented, but Courtney was dealt a second blow later that year when Kristin Pfaff was also found dead, in her case from a drugs overdose. Suddenly, the trauma and heartbreak of *Live Through This* seemed horribly real, and it promptly sold over 500,000 copies. Melissa Auf Der Maur, a composed and talented bassist, was brought in to replace Pfaff, but Courtney was falling apart. Desperately unhappy, she immersed herself in self-abuse, and staggered helplessly about the stage during her gig at the UK's Reading Festival. At the MTV Awards, she asked her friend Michael Stipe (singer with R.E.M.) if he would promise to look after Frances if anything were to happen to her. Stipe refused, suspecting that compliance would encourage Courtney to kill herself.

In 1995, Courtney's troubles were largely behind her. Still causing outrage she has nevertheless proved herself strong enough to further her own, immensely successful career. Hole scored two major hit singles, helped by two brilliant videos for 'Doll Parts' and 'Violet'. With Melissa providing a wonderful sense of stability, Hole have toured extensively, selling out everywhere. Touring culminated in a triumphant return to the Reading Festival, where an evidently high-spirited Courtney refused to leave the stage.

Though many parents may be anguished at the idea, Courtney Love is not merely Seattle royalty, but a most significant female role model. Regardless of her history of excess, she has proved beyond any doubt that women can offer the rock world much that male bands never could. She has proved that it is not necessary to sacrifice femininity to achieve aggression and heaviness. Rather, her compelling career has opened the door for many similarly talented women.

Guitarist Eric Erlandson

hole

DRAIN

The ascendancy of Swedish band Drain is further proof of the enormous progress made by women within the rock spectrum. Drain, a talented all-female band, have never allowed their career to be overseen or controlled by external forces. The foursome are intelligent and determined enough to have broken through on their own terms.

Drain, who consist of vocalist Maria Sjoholm, guitarist Flavia Canel, bassist Anna Kjellberg and drummer Martina Axen, play an immaculate brand of post-grunge, mingling contemporary influences such as Alice In Chains and Soundgarden with powerhouse musicianship and irresistible melodies. They're one of the most exciting metal bands ever to have come out of Scandinavia, and whilst it is tempting to say that they've beaten the boys at their own game, it would also be missing the point.

'All we want to do is make music,' says Martina. 'Being in an all-female band, everyone expects us to make statements, but that's not what we're in this for. It would be great to think that both guys and girls appreciate us for our music, and not look on us as being "that girl band from Sweden".'

'People can't resist making an issue of it,' adds Anna. 'The only reason is that there are still so few women in rock. If there was a band consisting only of chimpanzees, people would probably treat them the same way.'

Along with Hole's Patty Schemel, Drain's Martina Axen is rapidly gaining respect for her drumming skills, although she remains one of an amazingly small number of women to have ever occupied a drum stool. Martina first picked up the sticks as a child living in Stockholm, and has been playing in bands with guitarist Flavia for twelve years. Anna became part of the band five years later, but the final line-up of Drain was not completed until 1993, when Maria Sjoholm auditioned for the singer's job.

'At no stage were we determined to have just women in the band,' explains Martina. 'We just recruited the best people for the job and took into account how well we all got along. When we were putting Drain together and were looking for a singer, we auditioned both guys and girls. Maria was the best singer that auditioned, and she fitted in with what we were doing straight away.'

Drain were signed by WEA Records, and in 1996 released the spectacular *Horror Wrestling*, an album which was to win them a broad and loyal fan base. With tracks like the accessible 'Serve the Shame', the brooding 'Smile' and the powerful, traumatic 'Stench', Drain demonstrated not only their talent but their own maturity. To succeed in a male-dominated environment, Drain have constantly been called upon to prove themselves, but their application to the task has turned them into a superbly professional outfit.

Anna: 'Not only in the music business, but in all business, there are really only males at the very top, so you get used to looking up to them and dealing with it. There's a lack of good role models for girls which certainly makes things a lot harder.'

'Whatever you do, even if you're just watching a movie,' says Martina, 'there's gonna be forty or fifty men in it, and maybe just four or five women passing through. It's like that in the music business sometimes. A film like *Thelma and Louise* comes along and everyone talks about it just because it comes from a different perspective. Then, in rock music, we come along, and everyone makes an issue of it.'

For a band who were once turned down by a booking agency purely for being all-female, and were rejected by a certain record company for exactly the same reason, Drain have maintained a refreshingly positive attitude to life and business alike.

'A lot of people expect us to be bitter, angry feminists, but we're not like that at all,' smiles Anna. 'Over the last ten years things have improved greatly for women. Nothing ever happens overnight, but every year attitudes are changing. Women are more in control of their lives and generally have more opportunities to do what they wanna do.'

An extensive tour with Fear Factory and Manhole has helped the band to establish themselves on European soil. They continue to work at a frightening pace, adding more live dates and writing a brace of new songs. This is one band who are going anywhere but down the drain.

l r Flavia Canel guitar, Maria Sjoholm vocals
Anna Kjellberg bass, Martina Axen drums

SKIN [SKUNK ANANSIE]

'You have to learn the art of survival. It's a question of beat up or get beaten up.'

Skunk Anansie's strong-willed vocalist Skin is reflecting on life on the streets of Brixton, the tough South London suburb where she was brought up. It was here, in a locality best known for its riots and racial tension, that the young Skin discovered the facts of life, and came to appreciate society's problems at an early age. Her background gave her an ideal grounding for the political rage and rapture of Skunk Anansie's superb debut, *Paranoid and Sunburnt*.

Black, bisexual and shaven-headed, Skin is not the kind of character traditionally welcomed into the white, male-dominated music industry's bosom. Skunk Anansie are a knife in the heart for the old-fashioned, deep seated attitudes that still linger. Skin is deeply committed, always enthusiastic and wise beyond her years. Frankly, she has had to be.

'When you've got someone like me fronting a band, everyone assumes that its gonna be very politically correct, and that people are gonna lap it up,' she says. 'The reality is that the way we are, and the way I am, have made things a lot more difficult. If we were a band of four white boys a lot of things would have come more easily. We've really had to fight for respect every step of the way, because a lot of people just won't accept women who have a voice. When we've stepped outside England, things have been even worse. A lot of people just can't deal with the idea of a black woman fronting a rock band.'

Life in Brixton turned Skin into a dedicated fighter, the sort of person who could take on the industry and make a difference. Fortunately for her, she enjoyed a stable family life, and was always encouraged to appreciate music. Her grandad ran a dance club, and her earliest musical memory is of sitting on the club's stairs watching people dancing to reggae and calypso music. As a teenager, her social conscience was pricked by the local council's black female leader, while her musical taste buds were being stimulated by the driving, energetic pop of Blondie and the Police.

'After university, I worked as an interior designer, but walked out when I discovered I could sing,' she recalls. 'I hit it off with Lee, our manager, after he'd seen me singing in a club. He knew a guy who could write songs, but I had realised from an early age that

Skin Skunk Anansie s debut wasn t the only thing to go gold in

if I was ever gonna break into rock, I'd have to learn to do most things myself. I didn't want to be in a position where anyone could tell me what to do. All women in rock need to have as much control over their career as possible.'

Skin put Skunk Anansie together in 1994, and effectively ran her own studio, even throwing in her housing benefit money. After some ferocious demo work, the group were signed to One Little Indian Records in August of that year. One Little Indian were by no means the only company to take an interest in the band, but Skin hadn't been prepared to compromise in the past, and she certainly wasn't going to start now. Over the next two years, Skunk Anansie toured with everyone from Killing Joke to Bon Jovi, enjoying a string of hit singles and a Top Ten album. Skin's sensitive side was revealed in tracks like 'Weak', an interesting counterpoint to the flame and fury of 'Selling Jesus' and 'Intellectualise My Blackness'. Those prepared to listen without prejudice were enthralled.

'Of course prejudice is still a problem,' admits Skin, 'but I think things are improving. Some people will hate us and others will love us, but there's a lot of female-fronted bands now that play good music and aren't based around being sexual. Sure, they're still sexual in a sense, but women in rock are no longer forced to wear mini-skirts and leather. Some female bands are quite tomboyish in their approach, so male fans don't go in with that 'get-yer-tits-out' mentality. Women are proving they can be strong, assertive and intelligent in their music. I think we're getting there, but there's still a long climb ahead.'

Unfortunately for pioneers like Skin, a so-called 'lad culture' has emerged in Britain, as a retort to the decade's surge for equality and tolerance.

'The lad element is really alarming. It's not so much the presence of the element itself, but the speed and enthusiasm with which it's been embraced. Once again, it's all based around sexism and intolerance. It's as if people are saying, "Great, we can be wankers again and get away with it."'

Skin believes that it would be naive to expect gender to ever stop being an issue. 'I'd like to be treated with the same respect as a man, but at the same time, I'd like people to respect the fact that I'm a woman. I'm not one of the boys. It's always been more acceptable for boys to form groups but that's just part of socialisation. Women are directed towards family matters and having babies. Furthermore, some of the press portray women rockers as either perpetually drunk and drugged up, or as cute and cuddlesome. Women in rock bands who have something to say are eventually condemned for having a mouth. You have to fight it, not worry about it. If you compromise you end up feeling suffocated.'

There has never been a personality in rock quite like Skunk Anansie's compelling leader. Black women have made their presence felt in almost all musical fields, but it is taking someone with the fortitude of Skin to break down rock's long-standing barriers. People who are perceived as 'different' are either persecuted for not fitting in, or change the attitudes of others by uprooting certain institutions, exposing them for the dinosaurs that they are. Skin is one of the latter, a prime mover on rock's evolutionary scale.

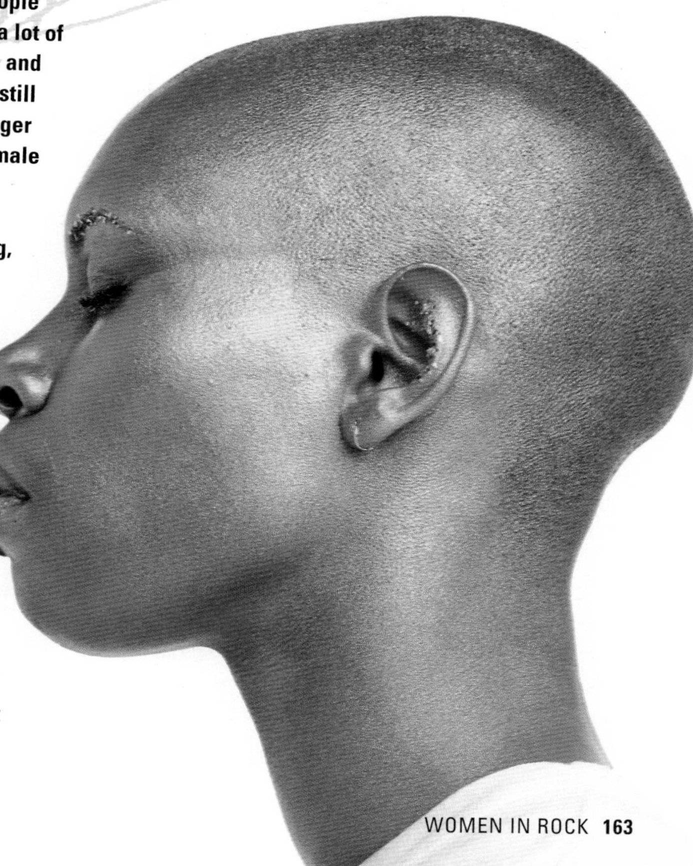

Sean Yseult officially became a person when she got into AC/DC and found herself hypnotised by Angus Young's bludgeoning guitar theatrics. It was witnessing this, rather than having a specific female role model, that made her want to form a band. At design school, she met Rob Zombie and put the first incarnation of White Zombie on the road. She even stole warning lights from the roadside to spell out the word 'Zombie' on stage.

'I've never really identified much with the idea of being a girl, except for the obvious fact that I am one,' she says, with a demonic giggle. 'Having said that, it isn't actually that obvious, and I seem to have been mistaken for a guy most of my life, but that's fine by me. The musicians that have been most inspiring to me have been people like Angus, Nikki Sixx and Gene Simmons, and the only females I can

Sean Yseult

White Zombie

On stage, White Zombie bassist Sean Yseult is a spastic blur of sound, colour and energy. Although she would cringe at the thought, she is among the most prominent of a new breed of female musicians in otherwise all-male bands. With characters like Sean and Smashing Pumpkins' bassist D'Arcy not only producing cutting edge music but also gaining widespread commercial acceptance, the role of rock star need no longer be purely male-occupied.

'I'm not resentful that gender is still treated as an issue, but I do find it rather annoying,' reveals Sean. 'All too often, women make mistakes and end up as their own worst enemies. I hate it when girls get together and form bands with names like Foxy. There isn't actually a band called that, but it's fairly typical. It's a really "girlie" name, and it immediately puts you into a little box. Guys don't do that. At least L7 are cool. They chose to play heavy music and they chose a name that didn't signify that they were all girls. I think that too many girls spend ninety-nine per cent of their time trying to draw attention to the fact that they are girls, and in doing so, forget to become a person.'

White Zombie

remember looking up to were Poison Ivy from the Cramps and Joan Jett.

'I first went to see Joan Jett in 1982, and I was attracted to her because she seemed to be like a female Ramone. Skinny, dark hair, dressed in black, jumpin' around, shrieking and playing the shit out of her guitar. Being a girl who spent most of my time wishing I was a guy, that was certainly inspiring.'

Sean's confidence was increased by the fact that White Zombie initially played gigs with a host of other bands whose line-up always seemed to include at least one woman. Zombie played with Honeymoon Killers, Pussy Galore and the Swans, and because no attention was ever drawn to the situation, prejudice never surfaced. Years on, with White Zombie co-headlining a U.S. tour with Pantera, Sean Yseult's presence in the band seems as natural as toast and jam.

'I try to be a musician first and a girl second,' she says. 'That in itself is a good thing for a young girl to see in society. I've never encountered prejudice because I've never invited it. I've never behaved like a stereotype. I think that the way I act within the sub-society that I belong to at least proves that there is more in life to aspire to than growing up, marrying a football player and having kids.'

Live Through This – ROCK LIFESTYLES

MONTE CONNER
A&R MAN

There are few more maligned record company roles than that of the A&R person. A&R people are responsible for signing up new talent and, in many cases, developing it once it has arrived. If you work in A&R, the chances are that you're inundated every day by mail bags full of demo tapes and invitations from bands to come and see them play. If you're employed by one of the really big companies, it's impossible to accept every invitation or to offer constructive criticism on every tape you receive. That's where the notorious 'standard rejection letter' comes in, leading to the popular misconception that A&R people are arrogant, over paid, ignorant individuals who simply don't care.

In fact, little could be further from the truth. Most A&R people do care immensely about new talent, but those with experience are healthily cautious and don't wish to over commit themselves. A company's A&R department is the teeth and jaws of its parent label's business. If you're going to develop a band and sell millions of their records, you obviously need to have something very special to start with, and the poor, misunderstood A&R man is under pressure to find that certain something.

One of the most successful seekers of new talent in recent years has been Monte Conner.

'What do I look for?' says Monte. 'Great songs. Great guitar players are a dime a dozen. The real talent in this business is to be able to write a great song that sticks in the head. I look for a certain uniqueness, great songs and lots of aggression.'

Monte Conner has never yet discovered a band simply by receiving a demo tape through the post. He believes that the best way for a band to get noticed by A&R fraternities is to develop a grass roots following and impress local media and DJs. The next stage is to persuade one of them to approach an A&R department on your behalf.

'Many A&R people won't even take unsolicited tapes,' warns Monte. 'Every band I've ever signed has come to me via some sort of music industry connection. No matter what town you're from, there's bound to be someone you can approach at a local radio station, someone at a club, someone at a magazine, someone that has connections to people at record companies. Every good A&R man has a nationwide network of contacts.'

For all his success, Monte Conner can still be found wading through hundreds and hundreds of unsolicited demo tapes every week.

'I can't resist it,' he sighs. 'There's always that niggling concern in your mind that the new Metallica might be in there somewhere. It hasn't happened yet, but there's no harm in looking!'

Monte Conner

DOMINIC DELUCA
SKATEBOARD SHOP OWNER, A&R MAN & TV PRESENTER

You can only guarantee one thing about rock and metal fashion, and that's the fact that it will never stop changing. Always expect the unexpected. In the seventies, people wore flared trousers and let their hair grow lank and long. The eighties started off with leather and lace, bullet belts and studded wristbands. It ended with bouffant hairstyles, make up, brightly coloured scarves and bandanas. The style that has epitomised the nineties perhaps more than any other is Grunge, supposedly an unequivocal rejection of everything that went on in the eighties, but in reality, nothing more than the latest uniform of youth.

In the nineties, young people are under more pressure than ever to conform with the fashions and styles of their heroes. The good thing is that wishing to conform is no longer an unrealistic aspiration. Pressure comes only from fads, and the speed at which things change. Nineties rock heroes like Soundgarden, Hole and Green Day do not look like bronzed, perfectly formed, super rich gods and goddesses. They look like real people, people you might meet on the streets or in clubs, people that you can identify with.

Former *Headbangers' Ball* presenter and talent scout Dominic DeLuca, knows more than most about ever changing rock fashions. His skateboard and streetwear store, situated in Brooklyn, is the target of many young people hoping to catch up with the latest fads and accessories. Surprisingly perhaps, Dominic has fastidiously resisted the temptation to follow trends.

'I was selling this gear long before it was trendy, but I'm not trying to change anyone,' he explains. 'I get a lot of customers asking me for certain brands that I won't stock because you can go into any shopping mall and find them. That's trendy; that's people trying to conform. If I was to sell that stuff, I'd do well initially, but once that trend ends, my store also ends.

'A lot of the bands that are really big now have been wearing this kinda gear for the last few years, and a lot of these streetwear companies would give bands like Anthrax and Offspring free clothing, because they know that the way bands look is always gonna influence the way kids wanna look. It's so extreme now that it can get kinda cheesy. Kids will come into my shop and buy a skateboard purely so they can walk around with it and look the part!'

As early as the fifties, boys were putting grease into their hair in an attempt to look like Elvis. Back then, it was more to do with rebellion than conformity. Kids didn't want to look like the future accountants and doctors that their parents wanted them to be. Nineties youth generally has more liberated parents (the same people who used to grease their hair in the fifties) and the emphasis is less on rebellion and more on staying up to date.

'Most rock 'n' roll people are very trendy,' notes Dominic. 'I remember being part of the hardcore scene in New York, a time when I'd always wear Doc Martens boots. I'd go to a club where I was working and where Warrant was playing. All the glam kids would give me a hard time for not wearing cowboy boots until, a few months later, Skid Row came along, all wearing Doc Martens. Next time I go to the same club, what's everyone wearing? Doc Martens! On Warrant's next album, what are *they* wearing? Doc Martens!!

'Fashion plays far too great a part in music today. When I was younger, people used to discover bands by trading tapes, reading magazines and going to millions of shows. Now people are fickle, brainwashed into constantly striving to be cool. Look at Green Day. They sold millions of copies of *Dookie*, but their next album only sold a quarter of that because the kids had been given a new band, Bush. In America, metal really suffered when *Headbangers' Ball* was taken off the air. The scene is no less huge, but it's dominated by fads and shortlived trends. But just look at the way it's going. Kiss, Van Halen and Mötley Crüe are all reforming. Marilyn Manson are doing well, and they're not alternative – they're metal. White Zombie is huge, and they're also metal. All these short haired people are probably gonna have to grow their hair long again!'

Dominic DeLuca is an unorthodox A&R man. He isn't content to sit in an office all day, wading through tapes and biogs. In fact, DeLuca wants nothing to do with that sort of thing.

'I'm not interested in listening to loads of demo tapes – I want to get out there and hang out, sample a band's vibe and find out whether they have grass roots support,' he enthuses. 'I've never yet found a band simply though listening to a tape. Ninety-nine per cent of tapes are garbage. All the bands I've signed have been discovered through contacts and recommendations.'

Rather than spending his time at the record label, he uses one of his skateboard stores as an office. By keeping everything relaxed and youth oriented, Dominic remains in touch with the bands that are considered to be happening.

'Some A&R people are over forty, and they're not necessarily the kind of people a young band would want to hang out with,' he concedes. 'I do things differently.

'When a band meets me, they discover that I'm like them: I skateboard, smoke dope, watch other bands and generally dig the lifestyle. It makes it so much easier for them to relate, and so much easier for me to know where to find the right bands.'

'I try to look for things that aren't so different that they're impossible to appreciate. I'm not necessarily looking for new sounds. I'm looking for the type of sound that I think the kids will go for, and as I'm one of those kids myself, I think I'm in the ideal position. I'm looking for a certain quality of sound, a certain kind of look, a band that gives you a rush of excitement. What I'll do is play a tape to a bunch of kids of eighteen to twenty years of age, and if we still dig it after that, I'll approach the record label's President with it. A&R is hard, because you're trying to please everybody. It's not easy for people who control record companies, people who are maybe in their forties or beyond, to appreciate what kids of fifteen regard as hip.'

A good A&R person is likely to form a strong allegiance to the artist he has signed. Everyone naturally wants their band to do well, but particularly keen A&R people will go above and beyond the call of duty to support their artists. Dominic is among the most fervent.

'If I sign a band, then it's my word and my friendship. There are no half measures. The bands I'm involved with aren't my clients; they're my friends. It hurts when you think a band is gonna be huge, and the people you work for don't agree. God knows, I'm not in this to make money. I get really passionate about it, and that's the most important thing.'

GLORIA CAVALERA

BAND MANAGER AND MOTHER

Saying that a band is only as good as their manager is an exaggeration, but only a small one. The manager is the man or woman who ties up all the loose ends, looking after the business interests of the group so that the band members themselves can get on with the preferred business of writing songs and performing. Managers come from all walks of life. An artist might start by recruiting a close friend to represent them in their formative years. Later, anyone with a go getting personality and a knowledge of the music industry is liable to make an effective manager. People with contacts in such fields as A&R, media and clubland are always going to be in demand by the stars of tomorrow.

Gloria Cavalera is among the most successful, and yet unorthodox, band managers of the decade. Since 1990 she has overseen the career of Sepultura, not only one of the most awesome metal bands of the nineties, but since Gloria's arrival on the scene, one of the most successful. Her relationship with the band is not strictly business, with Gloria preferring to view the band as an extension of her family. After all, she did marry one of them!

'I'm very fortunate to have so much support from my husband, Max,' she says. 'The rest of the band are also very patient, tolerant people to work with. There's a real family spirit present in the entire operation. Even the crew, who we've stuck with virtually from day one, are treated as part of the family.'

For three years Gloria ran a metal club in Phoenix, Arizona, putting on local bands like Sacred Reich, and opening the doors to kids of all ages. It was at a time when your club was likely to be closed down if it was known you were catering for metal kids, and Gloria was soon drawn into management, firstly looking after Sacred Reich. At first she was overwhelmed at the concept of band management, but quickly realised that her clubland background had provided her with all the necessary grounding.

The career paths of Gloria and Sepultura, that were to become so fortuitously entwined, first crossed on 31 October 1989, when the Brazilian mayhem merchants were opening for Sacred Reich at the New York Ritz.

'Although none of them except Max really spoke much English, I went to see them again in Phoenix, and agreed there and then to work with them,' she recalls. 'Before I made a firm commitment, however, I went out on tour with them just to make sure we'd be able to get on with each other. I'm unlike other managers in that respect. I like to have a relationship that's personal, not just career minded.'

Under Gloria's guidance, Sepultura's career began to move in all the right directions. Gradually, Gloria's role changed from pushing the band into the industry's face to protecting them from the very same people.

Max Cavalera
Sepultura

'Now that Sepultura are so big, I'm always having to stand up for their interests and integrity. For example, it's natural for a record company to want their biggest band to write a radio friendly song, but with Sepultura, that will never happen. It's not what they're about. Luckily, the label have never pushed us on that, although it's been hinted a couple of times!'

So successful has Gloria's management career been, it's often easy to forget that she is also a dedicated family lady with many commitments away from the band. Not only does she have her career and that of Sepultura to worry about, but she is also the proud mother of seven children.

'I had five children already when I met Sepultura, and those children trained me to deal with the members of the band,' she laughs. 'You get used to life being full of surprises. I'm fortunate in that Max and I are married, because it makes it a lot easier to take the kids with us on the road. If we left them at home, particularly the younger ones, they probably wouldn't know us when we came back. It *is* difficult at times though, especially for me. I've been known to go into meetings carrying the baby, or to put down important phone calls because someone's sliced their finger open!'

Sleep is something that Gloria Cavalera can live without, which is fortunate when you consider that she has the type of working schedule that would steer most of us towards a nervous breakdown.

'I get up at about 4.30 in the morning, and go through till about midnight,' she says casually, as if everyone lives by such a routine. 'Other than being the band's manager, I have to arrange things for them like the buying of their houses and setting them up with green cards, visas and bank accounts. I'm involved in all aspects of their international life.

'I've always followed my gut instinct and listened to logic. The one gift I was born with was the ability to pull a lot of things together in an organised manner. I couldn't write a song for Sepultura if my life depended on it, but I can organise people and make things work. Vanessa Warwick of *Headbangers' Ball* once said that I have a reputation for being hard but fair, and I really liked that. Consider me a fifth band member!'

ANDY COPPING
MUSIC AND CLUB PROMOTER

If Andy Copping ruled the world, at least the beer would be free. The Lincolnshire born DJ turned music and club promoter is the court jester and crown prince of Britain's rock/metal clubland all rolled into one. Copping is a name synonymous with loud music, flowing beer, band promotions and giveaways, and the most well attended rock nights anywhere in the country. Some of these nights, often co-promoted by MTV's *Headbangers Ball*, are now legendary.

'In 1995, we got together with MTV for what has certainly been the biggest organised event we've ever put on,' reflects Andy. 'It was the legendary *Headbangers' Ball* Donington party, right here at XLs in Birmingham!

'Everyone was telling us we'd never pull it off, but we knew better. All the Donington bands – Metallica, White Zombie, Warrior Soul, etc – all came down after the show. It was *immense.* Some of the bands mingled with the club goers, others did guest DJing, and Slayer served cocktails behind the bar. *Headbangers' Ball* were on hand to record the lot. To actually go into a rock club and see Metallica sat there drinking is outrageous, but that's exactly what happened.'

The *Headbangers' Ball* Donington party has been the pinnacle of Andy Copping's spectacular career, which has seen him rise from being a small time DJ in Lincoln to his current standing as the kingpin of slammin' rock nights throughout the country. The young Copping was, as he is now, a rabid fan of rock music. He got into DJing purely on account of his fabulously large album collection. He made his name at Nottingham's now famous Rock City, quickly transforming it from being just a very big rock club into the best in the country.

Having started as the club's DJ, he then began booking bands and promoting the club, soon winning the respect of MTV, record companies and the music press.

'My name was also growing within the industry as a whole, so I set up my own promotions company,' he explains. 'As a DJ, you get sent loads of new product from record companies, as well as promotional materials. I felt that a lot of it could be handled better, so I started organising special promotional launch nights myself at different clubs around the country.

'Punters are expecting a lot more out of rock clubs today, They can go to a club and hear an album in advance of its release. We also give away free T-shirts, together with sampler CDs, posters and so on. The kids are getting this as a supplement to what they'd normally get at a rock club. Everyone benefits, from the record company to the club to the kids.'

Needless to say, as the genre of rock music has moved ever onwards, it has continually changed and shed its skin over the years. For people like Andy Copping, staying on top of the prevailing trends is utterly essential in maintaining a rock club's credibility and popularity. In the late eighties, Andy helped to make Rock City a mecca for glam rock. As the years passed, and rock went from glam to grunge, Andy was obliged to change the emphasis of his rock nights.

'It's changed enormously over the last six years. As the manager of a club the problem is that some of your punters are still back in the lipstick and eyeliner era, which is fine if that's what they want, but it's certainly a head-ache for the DJ. Now things are moving around again – it's gone away from angst and gloom to bands like Green Day and The Wildhearts, fun bands with an "alternative" edge.'

Andy Copping

'I've got to be aware of what's going on, and a good way of doing that is to get involved with MTV and *Headbangers' Ball*. They've wanted to get right to the forefront of the club scene and put something back in. MTV have been heavily involved with various events we've put on. As well as the famous Donington party at XLs, we've co-promoted a "Beach Party" at Nottingham Rock City, which was a roaring success. Loads of stars came along, kids dressed down in beachwear, and it was a great laugh.'

'After that, MTV had a Christmas party down in London, which was tied in with Machine Head, who were the band of the moment. Everyone went absolutely bananas. A natural successor to that was our Fear Factory End of Tour Party, here at XLs, once again in association with *Headbangers' Ball*. All the band came down, we had Sony playstations set up around the place, tons of freebies, and a vodka promotion which ended up killing half the kids. At least thirty had to carried out of the club – oops!'

Andy Copping's rock nights are quite rightly the stuff of legend, particularly when they're spiced up by MTV inspired themes and activities, or record company promotions. Like most people who have managed to stay on top of it all, Andy maintains a seamless love and dedication to the world of heavy music. He'll just have to reconsider the cheap vodka in future!

'Yes, I'm a businessman, but only in the sense that I have to find out what the kids are into. It may sound like a cliche, but the fact is that I still remain a total one-hundred percent fan of rock music. If I hear a brilliant new album I can feel the hairs on the back of my neck standing up. This job still gives me chills!'

THE FANZINE WRITERS

For every band featured on *Headbangers' Ball*, or in the national rock press, there are a hundred that aren't. For every style of music that is considered to be fashionable, there is another that is struggling for survival. It's here that fanzines, independently produced magazines written by fans for fans, can play a part.

Shari

In covering the underground scene, music that is often dismissed as irrelevant by the mainstream media, fanzines provide a vital service for both artists and enthusiasts. There is also no limit to the types of presentation or narrative angles that a fanzine writer may choose to employ. *Blackout*, for example, offered a mix of rock related features and comic strips, while the sadly defunct *Rock's Off* provided a platform for editor Darren Stockford to express his anger and disillusionment at the music business.

Shari

Above all, a good fanzine is a shining example of supreme dedication to a cause. *Black Velvet* editor Shari has kept a fire burning for glam rock for the last two years. Though not exclusively dedicated to glam bands, *Black Velvet* nevertheless provides a haven for fans who have seen their particular genre spat on and ignored by every other outlet.

'I've always loved glam, and I will keep pushing it as much as I can,' she says. 'I've never been musically talented myself, but I had a flair for writing and decided I'd give it a shot. There are still lots of people who support this type of music, and miss its heyday. People are amazingly loyal. A lot of bands that I cover wouldn't have a chance of being featured elsewhere.'

Shari herself is an ardent Bon Jovi fan, and has attended over seventy-five Jovi concerts all over the world. She has resisted the temptation to turn *Black Velvet* into a tribute to her heroes, instead preferring to support new talent.

'A fanzine's main strength is that of providing a new band with a starting point,' she explains. 'It'd be great to do a Bon Jovi 'zine, but they're so well covered elsewhere.'

Two of the finest fanzines currently available in the UK are *Hard Roxx*, run by husband and wife team Matt and Kim Honey, and *Frontiers*, operated by Mark Foster. Both began by covering the much maligned melodic rock genre, but have constantly expanded and improved their output.

'Music goes around in cycles, and there will always be a demand for music that isn't covered by the mainstream media,' says Kim Honey. 'The demand for fanzines increases when the mainstream media move away from the music that people have supported for years, and those people are desperate for news and coverage of their favourite bands. Suddenly, a whole new market opens up.

'For some bizarre reason, our readership becomes more prevalent the further north you go. New readers come over to us all the time, perhaps because they hear we've got a Slayer interview, or an article on Honeycrack. Sebastian Bach of Skid Row is our most famous reader, and he's actually become the magazine's honorary president!'

Mark Foster launched *Frontiers* as a riposte to what he saw as a disintegrating rock media. It is now bi-monthly and can boast a readership of over 3,500. Foster has even come close to a retail deal with WH Smith.

'Rather then slagging off rock magazines all the time, we decided we'd do something about it,' he says. 'These days, a band has to be signed to a major label or wearing trendy gear to have any chance of mainstream coverage. Fanzines are prepared to look for what's bubbling under the surface, and champion the underdog.

'It may sound idealistic, but I still believe there's room for a magazine that doesn't take any judgmental stance on what's hip and what's not. It should be up to the reader to decide what they're gonna go for. Right now, there's a danger of magazines and writers taking on more importance in their own minds than the bands they're actually writing about!'

Many of today's fanzine writers are tomorrow's newspaper columnists or magazine editors. They remain an essential part of the rock media's infrastructure. Fanzines offer bands an opportunity to make their name known to the real enthusiasts, the people that actually buy records and demo tapes and go to gigs. They also allow entire marginalised genres to have a voice and an outlet. Without fanzines, and the dedication of those that create them, rock's very roots would be in danger of decay.

Further information

Black Velvet: 336 Birchfield Road, Webheath, Redditch, Worcestershire, B97 4NG. Send £1 and A4 SAE. Cheques payable to 'S.Green'.

Hard Roxx: 14 Stoats Nest Road, Coulsdon, Surrey, CR5 2JD. Costs £2. Cheques payable to 'K.Honey'.

Frontiers: 11 Robson Drive, Aylesford, Kent, ME20 7JR. Costs £2.95. Cheques payable to 'IDC Ltd'.

MAURICE JONES
CONCERT PROMOTER

For British rock fans, Christmas usually comes on the third or fourth Saturday in August. The Monsters of Rock festival at Castle Donington in Derbyshire is the biggest event on the rock calender, an almost annual institution that has only grown in scale over the years. Donington's promoters have rarely failed to put together a bill that covers all of rock's many distanced boundaries, and have usually sold tickets by the truckload.

1996 brought together a reformed Kiss, plus the legendary Ozzy Osbourne, and a host of rising stars including Sepultura, Dog Eat Dog, Paradise Lost and Korn. Such a bill does not come together overnight and is not organised by just anyone. At Monsters of Rock, the buck stops with Maurice Jones.

'I'm not answerable to any kind of governing body,' says Jones, 'but out of courtesy I do discuss my intended bill with the headline artist. They have a large say in the way the bill is put together because they have their own musical integrity to think of. They may not always get things their own way, but I certainly pay careful attention to them. For example, Sharon Osbourne (Ozzy's wife and manager) recommended Dog Eat Dog for the 1996 bill, and also suggested we have Sepultura, who had been supporting Ozzy in the States. Bands establish friendships on tour which they like to carry over to the big events.'

Maurice Jones is an old hand in a relatively young business. He first took an interest in music in the sixties, initially managing bands, before going into business full time at the age of nineteen. Having learned his trade in the very earliest days of concert promotions, Jones went on to work with everyone from Simply Red to Oasis to AC/DC. His crowning glory came in 1985, when he co-promoted the massive Live-Aid spectacle with Harvey Goldsmith, helping to raise over $70 million for famine relief.

It is for Donington, however, that most rock fans will have reason to thank Maurice Jones. The logistics of staging such a metalfest are immense.

'I have to start thinking about the following year's bill even before the present year's show has taken place,' he muses. 'It's a job that goes on throughout the year. The most important thing to come up with is a suitable headline band. After that, you need another big name to go second on the bill, and the rest is relatively easy.'

In the eighties, finding the ideal bill topper was rarely problematic, but the nineties, and the diversification of rock music, poses new questions.

'What has happened is that a lot of bands have reached a certain level, but that certain level does not make them a true headliner. The music industry has changed immeasurably as far as rock goes. I'm certain that it will change again, but right now it's really making life difficult. If we don't find a suitable headliner, we don't have a show. Simple as that. I wouldn't consider putting on a smaller show in Donington's place because the infrastructure would still be really expensive.'

Once the bill is established, the main priority of the promoter is to stage the event as spectacularly and successfully as possible. To do that, Jones must liaise closely with the headliners in the run up to the event.

'The stage is tailor made each year to the requirements of the headline band,' he explains. 'We need to know all the technical details of what exactly is going to happen. Otherwise we could end up with a stage that is too narrow for the band's lighting trusses, or they may need things like thrusts and walkways. The main band generally has a full production, but in the case of Kiss and Ozzy Osbourne we had a situation where both artists brought their full touring production sets in, the intention being to put on a full stage show for both acts.'

Maurice Jones is disarmingly modest about the skills that have helped him reach his current status. It's all about being able to add up, he reckons!

'Basically, you need to know the commercial appeal of your artist. A good start is to pick up on a small band in your local area and work some shows with them. It's easy to lose money, but as long as you can add up, it's surprisingly simple. You start with *x*, and you need to end up with *x plus*. You're bound to get *x minuses* but get too many and you're out of business!'

IAN DANTER
KISS FAN

You can count on the fingers of one hand the number of bands who can equal Kiss when it comes to fanbase loyalty. Kiss fans not only go to concerts, buy records and T-shirts, but are part and parcel of a thriving cottage industry. With conventions, fanzines and endless numbers of clubs and societies, some official and some not so official, there is a near religious fervour that seems to elevate Kiss beyond the level of mortality. Of all Kiss fans, there can be few more dedicated to the cause than 28-year-old Ian Danter from Birmingham.

As soon as you enter Danter's house, you are aware of the man's dedication to Messrs Stanley, Simmons, Frehley and Criss. Posters of the band, in their stack-heeled pseudo space-age glory, stare down at you from walls. The magnificent leather bound *Kiss-story*, a document Ian shelled out £150 for, has pride of place on the coffee table. Most impressive of all, a full-size Kiss pinball machine sits invitingly next to the kitchen door. It's been kept in immaculate condition. Go upstairs and you find framed polished collections of Kiss photos, plus enlarged snapshoots of Ian himself with various members of the group.

'I was about ten when I first took an interest in Kiss,' muses Ian. 'My elder cousin used to have a huge collection of rock albums, and I'd always enjoy flicking through them, fascinated by the artwork. Finally, I asked to borrow *Alive* by Kiss, and once I'd heard that first side of music I was drawn in – completely hooked. In fact, three weeks went by before I played the rest of the album because I was so fascinated by what I'd already heard!

'The appeal of the band is all encompassing. I think that the image and the management of that image has a lot to do with maintaining their mystique. You have to admire the conviction and the sheer bravado of the band. They never hold anything back.'

Ian owns four elaborate, professionally spray-arted T-shirts depicting each individual band member, plus two others depicting past members Eric Carr and Vinnie Vincent. As a teenager, he became obsessed with both Kiss' music and Kiss memorabilia, which led to a more general interest in music. He learned to play drums and guitar as an indirect result of his fascination.

'As far as the memorabilia goes, it was easy to see why there's such interest in it,' he laughs. 'A Kiss pinball machine seems like the most natural thing in the world while an Oasis pinball machine would be a horrible, naff gimmick. I won my pinball machine in a raffle at one of the Kiss conventions. The Kiss Fan Club, who were holding the raffle, tried to buy it back off me for £500, but I was having none of that. It's very rare and is worth many times that amount, although I could never part with it no matter what offer I might be made.

'The memorabilia gets crazier and crazier. The band don't approve of all of it. There are now Kiss phone cards which are quite collectible, and there used to be bubblegum cards and even a Kiss 'On Tour'

A rather pleased Ian Danter centre meets Gene Simmons left and Paul Stanley of Kiss

board game. In the heyday you could've got bendy dolls, pens, lunchboxes, even a Kiss wigwam. You could even bonk the object of your desire with a Kiss condom if you'd wanted!'

Needless to say, Danter owns every Kiss album that has ever been released, plus a few that were never officially released at all. He cites *Alive* as his all time favourite, an unsurprising choice considering that the entire course of his life was changed by it.

'After that, I'd pick *Destroyer*,' he continues. 'It was years ahead of its time and was a real diversion from the previous albums. To go from songs like 'Rock And Roll All Nite' to things like 'Beth' and 'Great Expectations' is one massive leap. Another favourite is 'Creatures Of The Night' because of the heaviness and intensity. The four solo albums are really under-rated, particularly those by Ace Frehley and Paul Stanley.'

For Ian Danter, the climax of his loyalty to Kiss came in 1992, when he finally got to meet his heroes. That memorable day simply encouraged Ian to go to greater lengths still. A few years later he casually walked into an exclusive hotel and managed to meet them again.

'The first time, I managed to sneak into their sound check session at the N.E.C. in Birmingham,' he recalls. 'Watching them practising the songs, and larking about was amazing enough. The most frightening moment was afterwards when Paul Stanley came walking down a ramp towards me. I froze. I can't tell you how it felt to finally meet him. It was the culmination of years of adulation on my part and influence on theirs – and here he was actually talking to me. It was hard to think of anything valid to say, but somehow I muddled through. I'm sure he just saw this gibbering wreck in front of him, and decided to take pity on me!'

This initial meeting was nothing compared to Danter's second encounter. He had heard that Kiss were staying at a certain hotel in London, and on further investigation had the chance to speak to them again, this time at length.

'The second time was much better,' grins Ian, 'although the build up was just as nerve shattering. This time I was able to sit down and just listen to them talk. I thought 'My God, here's Paul Stanley sitting two feet away from me telling me I look like Steve Harris from Iron Maiden, and here's Gene Simmons commenting on my customized Eric Carr T-shirt. It was mad, just mad. Gene even jokingly asked me to join the band at one stage!'

For their 1996-97 World Tour, Kiss reformed their original line-up and offered fans a chance to relive those heady days of the late seventies. It gave younger fans like Ian an opportunity to see the classic Kiss without the use of a time machine. The last time Kiss toured in this format, parental opposition barred the then twelve year old Ian from going to any of the shows. In the nineties, Danter finally had the chance to put that pre-teen anguish behind him. His eyes light up at the memory.

'The recent European dates have been the most spectacular ever,' he says. 'My cousin would constantly talk about seeing the original Kiss back in 1976, and I never imagined I'd get the chance to witness a similar thing. They've obviously worked very hard to make every aspect of their show as authentic as it could be. The irony is that, technically speaking, Kiss are more popular now than during their so-called heyday. The European shows of '96 and '97 were just spectacular. It looks like they've come back to defend their title!'

Stanley and Simmons live

PICTURE ACKNOWLEDGEMENTS

All pictures © Ross Halfin apart from:
pages 8 (Nine Inch Nails), 9 (Courtney Love), 24 (Nine Inch Nails), 25 (Courtney Love), 126, 127, 142, 143, 158, 159 © Tony Woolliscroft, pages 9, 134, 135, 150, 151 © MTV Europe, page 149 © Alchemy, page 166 courtesy of Monte Conner, 170 courtesy of Andy Copping, 171 courtesy of Shari, 174 courtesy of Ian Danter.